Angel Decoding

Secret Keys to Communicating
with Your Angels

MARIA GURNEY PETH, PHD

BALBOA.
PRESS
A DIVISION OF HAY HOUSE

Cover photo by Jennifer Meyer (Forever Now Photography)
Author photo by Karmen Wilder (Karmen's Studio)
Editor Chandler Tyrrell (Wordstream LLC)

Balboa Press books may be ordered through booksellers or by contacting:

Balboa Press
A Division of Hay House
1663 Liberty Drive
Bloomington, IN 47403
www.balboapress.com
1-(877) 407-4847

Because of the dynamic nature of the Internet, any web addresses or links contained in
this book may have changed since publication and may no longer be valid. The views
expressed in this work are solely those of the author and do not necessarily reflect the
views of the publisher, and the publisher hereby disclaims any responsibility for them.

The author of this book does not dispense medical advice or prescribe the use of any
technique as a form of treatment for physical, emotional, or medical problems without the
advice of a physician, either directly or indirectly. The intent of the author is only to offer
information of a general nature to help you in your quest for emotional and spiritual well-
being. In the event you use any of the information in this book for yourself, which is your
constitutional right, the author and the publisher assume no responsibility for your actions.

ISBN: 978-1-4525-7354-0 (sc)
ISBN: 978-1-4525-7356-4 (hc)
ISBN: 978-1-4525-7355-7 (e)

Library of Congress Control Number: 2013907791

Printed in the United States of America.

Balboa Press rev. date: 5/8/2013

CONTENTS

Acknowledgments and Appreciation...................................v

Introduction   What Is Angel Decoding? vii

Chapter 1   Devotion: The Key to Intuition 1

Chapter 2   Know Your Angels................................. 11

Chapter 3   Hear Your Angels................................... 21

Chapter 4   I Heard the Angels Speak 27

Chapter 5   Born Knowing....................................... 41

Chapter 6   Vibration at the Rate of Love.................. 49

Chapter 7   Emotional Intelligence 55

Chapter 8   More Than the Eye Can See 65

Chapter 9   On a Mission.. 79

Epilogue   Final Ponderings 81

Appendix   Aura Colors: A Basic Guide 84

About the Author.. 92

Acknowledgments
and Appreciation

I am eternally grateful to God, our precious Creator, the power of the Holy Spirit, and the loving angels.

I am living a blessed life filled with abundance and life-affirming experiences because of the many people who touched my life as teachers, students, clients, and friends. I am ever grateful for my loving family, whose encouragement has made a deep impression in my soul.

Many people contributed to this book. I want to thank all those who shared with me their intimate experiences with spirit and the teachers, clients, and students who helped shape my ideas and contributed to the concepts developed in this book.

My special thanks to the diligence of the early previewers who took the time to read and share their ideas: Jackie Gurney, Mary Peth, Leslie Allison Kebschull, Whitney Marie Judas, Wendi Schirvar, Julie Walor, Gabi Danielson, Peter A. Gurney, and Rachel M. Peth.

To my husband Richard, son Derek, and daughter Rachel—
you are the lights of my life and the center of my universe.

God bless you all. I will never forget
your kindness to me.

INTRODUCTION

What Is Angel Decoding?

Have you ever found yourself wondering what your true purpose in life is? Or perhaps you're trying to figure out why you keep seeing, hearing, or encountering the same numbers or symbols over and over again? Angel decoding is a method of learning to comprehend and give meaning to the intuitive messages you receive; it is a means of angel communication. Scientific studies show that intuition is an inherent characteristic of the human race. Learning to decode and comprehend the messages angels are conveying is an amazingly fun and easy skill. All you need is an open mind, a loving heart, a little guidance, and some practice, and you will be discerning and demystifying angelic messages in no time.

As a young child in Sao Paulo, Brazil, I found peace and friendship among my angels and spirit guides. For several years, I was separated from my mother, beginning at the age of three. My brave, young mother left me in the care of my grandmother and her eldest sister in order to travel to America to find a better life for us. In the early 1960s, telephones were not a standard feature in every South American home, so calling my mother, who lived more than five thousand miles away, was a rarity.

Our household consisted of my aunt Geny, my grandmother, and me. The three of us lived in a sparse but tidy, two-bedroom apartment. Lacking playmates and toys, I spent hours talking to my angels. I didn't know they were angels; I saw them as sparkles of rainbow light—like beams from the sun—and felt them as cuddly sensations of energy. I felt safe, happy, and peaceful when I played with these loving angelic lights.

Raised a devout Catholic, I recall pictures of Jesus and Mother Mary, as well as a crucifix, hanging on the walls of our tiny apartment. Every Sunday, we dressed in our best clothes for church and walked a couple of miles to a church, where we sat through a tireless, two-hour mass. My aunt and grandmother taught me to pray every morning and every night. Sometimes we would pray the rosary, sometimes we would talk to Jesus, but more often, we spoke to God. I learned that angels are always around us and that each of us is blessed with a guardian angel. I told my aunt several times that I played with the angels when she was gone to work all day, and she smiled and said, "Good." I am sure she was just humoring me, but her positive response was all the encouragement I needed to keep myself entertained by the beautiful, sparkly lights that comforted me each day.

I believe angels are assigned to us at birth, when God stated to our little souls, "Here is a part of me to always to be with you." Then the angels follow us out into this vast world, promising to support, guide, and encourage us whenever we ask. In faith, we are to pray to God and give all the glory to the Lord, but we are to ask the angels—God's messengers—for help. The angels need our permission in order to intervene on our behalf; they are bound to honor our free will. So I say, willingly ask your angels to support you in all you do and dream of, and then the angels will have free rein to carry you through life's challenges, opportunities, and dilemmas. Throughout my years, I have called on my angels to help me make important decisions and to send healing, courage, and love to other people. I have called on them to protect my loved ones and to bring miracles to those who are open and faithful.

Every one of us can pray and set an intention for an important outcome. We are unlimited creative beings of exceptional ability. Often, learning how to tap into our abilities and talents takes a bit of coaxing. With the right circumstance, teacher, or synchronistic opportunity, we can each find ourselves encountering a new discovery about our skills and spiritual gifts. Yes, angel decoding can be considered a spiritual gift—a gift you can tap into with the help of this book and some practice.

I believe we are all capable of communicating with our guardian angels and soul guides. I have witnessed numerous people realize the ability of greater intuition and angel communication during my workshops, often within a few hours time. I teach that learning how to communicate with angels is similar to learning how to read. The angels begin to help you build a glossary of symbols, impressions, awareness, and sensations. You need only to pay attention to the subtle messages and lessons from your angels in order to build your own angel-decoding lexicon/glossary. Once you learn to discern the gentle messages from your angels and guides, you will realize what an incredible gift of guidance and support your intuition can be. Living in joy, purposeful and aligned with God's greatest intentions, is a blessing indeed!

A First Lesson ~ The Power of Love and Connection

On the day of my fourth birthday, I was really missing my mother. "Where can I find my mama?" I asked my grandmother, my dear Vovo. Tears filled my eyes and spilled over, tracing the hollows of my cheekbones. Vovo reached out to touch my cheek and wipe away the tears, and then she put her plump arms around me and tenderly kissed my forehead. Cradled safely in my grandmother's arms, I recall listening intently as she shared an amazing secret of connecting intuitively with another person across great distances. My Vovo said, "Don't cry, my sweet child. The ones we love are always with us in our heart. Now, take a deep breath, and as you do so, hold your hands to your heart." I did as she suggested, and it felt as if I were starting on a kind of journey. With my hands to my heart, I snuggled in closer to Vovo. I took another deep breath and felt calm and excited all at once. Then she said, "Close your eyes and picture your mama. Pretend she is so close you can see her bright, brown eyes and can touch her face. Now keep repeating 'Mama' to yourself as you sense the love from her heart unite with your own. Experience her as if she is right beside you, and you will know how she is feeling in this very moment. If you take another breath, you can even understand what she is thinking. It's as if she is right here with you, inside your own mind and heart."

That day, I learned the lesson of a lifetime. It was my first intuitive experience, and I have continued to build my emotional quotient ever since. Perhaps it was childlike wonder or innocence; conceivably, it was God's blessing on my life in a teachable moment. What we learn willingly and experience deeply is remembered and imbued within us forever. From that day forward, I practiced the exercise numerous times a day. It was several years before I set eyes on my mother again, yet beginning with the moment when I learned to connect with her through my heart, I seldom felt deprived of her love and essence. To this day, I call upon the skill to connect emotionally across extended distances in order to "check in" with those I love and care about.

You can learn this method too, this strategy for messaging through the angel network. It's as if we are dialing into a private channel reserved by angels, allowing us to reach anyone we love on the other end of the line. A high-frequency channel accessed through the power of love and the essence of pure intention. It is an energy frequency reserved for each of us with the greatest of intentions, through a channel of love and light.

Angel Decoding is filled with actual applied and tested methods of intuitive awareness as I have taught them in my workshops over the last twelve years. Hundreds of people can attest to their success in using these strategies and the life-changing results they have achieved. The book's title emphasizes the skill of decoding, similar to the decoding we use when learning to read. By engaging and utilizing our six senses, we can make communication with the angels a breeze. *Angel Decoding* highlights ten key concepts (which are detailed below) certain to capture the attention of the spiritually minded person and win the hearts of the angel lover.

With passion, I set out to directly guide you—the reader—toward a deeper understanding of your true perceptive self, to inspire and challenge you to move toward an authentically intuitive life with full use of your sensory potential. Establishing a clear connection with the divine is key to opening a clear path to your life's purpose. Outcomes include an insurgence of confidence as capacities blossom and, in turn, transform the way you make decisions, view goals, and assess life. Whether you are searching for deeper meaning and direction in life or are simply interested in angels, you will find it easy to open your heart and soul to the lessons in this book, *Angel Decoding: Secret Keys to Communicating with Your Angels*.

I offer this breakthrough concept for decoding and demystifying angel communication because I believe each of us, when given the right tools and instructions, harbors the ability to effectively communicate with the angels. It truly is like learning to read.

Ten Angel-Decoding Secret Keys to Angel Communication

Angel-Decoding Secret Key #1 (Chapter 2)

> Love: express love, feel love, be loved, know love, share love, reflect love, embrace love.

Angel-Decoding Secret Key #2 (Chapter 2)

> Prayer, devotion, and meditation are the groundwork of success.

Angel-Decoding Secret Key #3 (Chapter 4)

> Learning to read the messages of divine consciousness requires good learning habits and practice.

Angel-Decoding Secret Key #4 (Chapter 5)

> Faith is to believe and know truth without understanding how you know.

Angel-Decoding Secret Key #5 (Chapter 6)

> It's not about you! Angel communication is about embracing purpose and seeing the grander vision of your mission as a soul.

Angel-Decoding Secret Key #6 (Chapter 6)

Heavenly angels always communicate through the high vibration of love. They want all the glory to go to God and are themselves a gift from God.

Angel-Decoding Secret Key #7 (Chapter 7)

Answers to your prayers begin with patience, trust, and faith, as prayerful devotion will grant clarity to the answers.

Angel-Decoding Secret Key #8 (Chapter 7)

The longer we are able to hold a positive thought and emotion, the more powerful the energy of the emotion becomes.

Angel-Decoding Secret Key # 9 (Chapter 8)

Angelic messages are always encouraging, consistent, and never hurtful. Angels will work to send you the same important message or answer you seek in many forms.

Angel-Decoding Secret Key #10 (Chapter 9)

To obey the logic of your soul is the only path you need. You are masterful beyond knowing; you only need to heed the music of your heart.

CHAPTER 1

Devotion: The Key to Intuition

Finally, I looked into my own heart and there I saw him;
he was nowhere else.

—Rumi

Everything you need to start the process of angel decoding is within you. Each of us on this amazing planet has been blessed with the extraordinary simply by being individuals. Being human makes us part of the unified field of love, and being individuals is our expression of that love in this world.

When you first learned to read, you were introduced to the alphabet. Getting grounded, spending a few minutes in meditation, and incorporating deep breathing into your daily life are the ABCs—the basic first steps—of creating a successful base upon which to build your skills in the process of angel decoding.

Success begins with preparation and practice. Angel decoding starts with devotion. I encourage you to begin and end each day by centering your breath to help establish balance and a deeper, higher vibration of your essence.

The Beginning of My Journey as Spiritual Teacher and Angel Therapist

On a crisp day back in 1999, I was in Minneapolis, Minnesota, sitting in a workshop given by Doreen Virtue, PhD. She had just guided the two hundred or so attendees through a mini angel-reading session. This was the first time I experienced my clairvoyant abilities clearly, and it was truly an aha moment. In an instant, I came to realize that what I had assumed for all the preceding years—that I was simply a good guesser—was wrong. A total stranger had just confirmed my true spiritual abilities, and I finally understood that I knew much more than the eye could see. My understanding reached beyond the physical and into the spiritual. Specifically, what I had done was use a variety of innate intuitive tools to give an accurate and helpful angel reading for my workshop partner. Later the same day, when I had time to reflect on the impact of that experience, I realized the inevitable: my life was clearly going to change. A part of me once masked was now emerging.

And so, with an open mind about what might happen next in my life, I did what had always come naturally to me when I needed answers and direction. I took deep, relaxing, and clearing breaths, and I said a prayer in my heart. I asked for direction from God and the angels as I surrendered to their guidance. The answer came to me a bit later that day.

But before I share that answer with you, I would like to take a few minutes to outline the process and the importance of breathing to attain a quiet mind in order to gain clarity and direction. Each one of us can access the guidance within by simply clearing our minds with a centering breath. Answers to baffling life questions are available to us if we are still and attentive. This method of opening ourselves to the path of awareness is within reach at any moment and in any place if we just breathe.

The Sacred Key: Centered Breath and Meditation

Every human life on earth begins with breath. Have you ever noticed how babies and young children breathe? When they breathe in, their tummies stick out, round and full like a beautiful Buddha belly. This happens because the lungs fill to capacity and the diaphragm expands downward and out toward the abdominal area. As we get older, we begin shortening our breaths, using less of our lung capacity for each typical breath. It is time to bring awareness to this deficiency and support a new practice of breathing, which in turn will support our health, balance our emotions, and help us tune into the guidance within. Breathing deeply and continuously opens the chest and heart—and when hearts are open, miracles occur.

What is more organic than breathing? We can live with minimal food, water, and clothing, but we cannot live more than a few minutes without oxygen. Breath *is* life. It can increase our sense of well-being, balance our energy centers, aid in releasing toxins at the cellular level, and boost brainpower. Imagine what you can do if you honor and utilize this gift with concentrated intention and practice.

I have found the following breathing exercise beneficial and easy to incorporate into my schedule. It combines practices and modalities from a variety of sources, including my own years of personal experience. When I relax into a centered position and breathe, I find that I can transcend distracting mind chatter and access higher states of consciousness. This is the place you want to journey to in order to more easily communicate with the angels.

Centered-Breath Exercise

Find a quiet space free of distractions where you can sit erect or lie flat on your back. Rest your arms and hands comfortably on your lap or, if you are lying down, alongside your body. If you are sitting in a chair, close your eyes, plant both feet flat on the floor, and imagine you are firmly grounded by Mother Earth.

Take a deep breath in through your nose and slowly count to four. At the same time, quiet your mind and allow yourself to be present and clear. Then exhale through your mouth, letting go of any stress and filling your heart center with love. Release any distracting mind chatter and focus instead on creating a sacred space within.

Continue taking these deep, cleansing breaths in through your nose and out through your mouth, inhaling and exhaling to the count of four. Focus on filling your lungs with life-giving oxygen while relaxing or softening the abdominal area so that you naturally extend your stomach as your diaphragm expands. This is called diaphragmatic breathing. Remember the breathing of little children, the way each breath fills them down to their tummies. Let your shoulders relax, let your arms and hands relax, and allow the stress to ooze out as you exhale.

Your work from this point forward is to breathe in and out smoothly, evenly, quietly, and deeply. Inhaling through the nose is healthier and more cleansing because your nose is a natural air filter. If your nose is stuffy, go ahead and breathe through your mouth as needed. Keep a steady pace of breathing as you empty your mind of intruding thoughts for a few moments.

Imagine the energy source surrounding you, holding you in a perfect space: aligned, clear, focused, safe, and supported. Be open to that place of pure intent, to that place of infinite attention to our divine parent. Truly experience your authentic self. Allow the thinking mind to step away, holding space for your pure essence.

In order to benefit from stress relief and the centering of your soul, you may need to incorporate a training strategy that allows your mind to go into a passive zone. Find a haven as you continue breathing peacefully. This is where you want to go for ten minutes. It is wonderful to give yourself permission to tune in to a tranquil silence. This is both healthy and often necessary for spiritual connection.

If you have trouble moving your pesky thoughts aside, focus on your breathing or count evenly as you breathe in and out. Either method is an excellent way to redirect your mind to peaceful solace. I have also found that resonating on a beautiful word can offer the same benefit. Focusing on a special word or phrase, called a mantra, is more typical of meditative practice, but it can offer similar benefits to centered breathing. I use the word *peace* to support my efforts to center and find that still, quiet place.

The fresh supply of oxygen that comes with each deep breath, as well as the calming of your body, will boost your brainpower and help lift your mood and level of happiness. There are multiple benefits to this practice, and they have been demonstrated as valid and included in research conducted by David Eisenberg, MD, and his colleagues at Harvard Medical School. They have proven that meditation can increase the activity of natural killer cells, which destroy bacteria, fungi, parasites, and cancer cells within the body, thus supporting the body's ability to remain healthy. Brain scans show increased levels of brain activity in the limbic system, the area of the brain that supports increased abstract visualization and more defined connections with our emotions. Increased emotional awareness is conducive to amplified intuition.

It has been proven that children score higher on cognitive tests and show longer levels of concentration after spending a few minutes taking deep breaths and holding their bodies in meditative postures. As a mother, I first encourage my children to take the time to breathe through a problem or issue when they face a dilemma. I prefer to teach my children methods of handling their problems in life with more focus and greater concentration and from a calm, peaceful, and centered place.

It is never too late or too early to start some form of centered breathing or other meditative exercise. This is why regular application of a meditative practice can and will change your life. I know that it has changed mine; I give centered breath a great deal of credit for my increased level of intuition and my success in life.

Angels Confirm My Destiny

On that day in 1999—the day I first truly recognized my spiritual gifts—I had already been using the centering-breath exercise for several years. When I used the exercise that day, it was to clear my mind and commune more openly with my soul. I had just completed my first successful angel reading only a few hours earlier. What I needed next was concentrated guidance from my angels on how to proceed with my life, so I centered through my breath and called on my angels and guides.

I was centering my breath, and the minutes were passing by, when I noticed that my head tingled with a peculiar sensation as I opened my heart for answers. In the following moments, I felt my loving angels' presence in a pronounced

7

manner. Since it had already been a day of important firsts, I welcomed this renewed sensation, this expanded feeling of awareness. I also experienced a vision—as if I was watching a short video clip in which I saw myself teaching other people to spiritually see, feel, hear, and know their angels. It was as if my guides and angels had knocked on my highest energy center—known as the Crown Chakra—and announced their presence and support for my efforts to move ahead on my spiritual path. In that moment, they got my attention and my gratitude—and to this day, they still have both.

Reflecting back to that day when the course of my life turned more intensely toward becoming a spiritual coach and teacher, I realized that I needed to move forward decisively with my soulful ability. I also understood that help was available and that my angels and guides would work through me to support the process. I would become a medium for messages of the divine. I would teach and support other people interested in improving their abilities and expanding their growth on the spiritual path.

A new Maria was born that day. I let go of fear and insecurity and limited ideas of who I was, and I accepted the mission of my soul's purpose. I am teacher, guide, and spirit. I am connected to God and to you, united in Holy Spirit, where we are truly in support of one another joined in unconditional love and fellowship.

Most days, we stumble around without purpose or direction in life, yet I left that weekend workshop with a new awareness. Trusting in God and starting every day with focused breath has taught me that I do not need every answer and that every day does not have to be completely outlined for me. Allowing source, spirit, angels, and guides to weave the cloth ahead of me is a much better choice.

Like most people, my daily schedule is busy, filled with the responsibilities of being a mother, wife, teacher, and an active contributor to my community. Yet when I am still and breathing through a problem or concern, grander answers come. The answer for the direction of my future became evident on that day in 1999, and I knew that I had changed because of my experience and the new awareness of my spiritual gifts. I am ever thankful for the clarity I received that day—and still receive today—from centering the mind and focusing on breath. Try it for yourself, and allow more miracles to manifest in your future.

Follow your daily expectations and attend to your responsibilities, yet allow for moments of quiet, breathing, and prayer to open yourself to transformation. Patience with this system of discovery and spiritual growth is necessary. Sometimes transitions occur very quickly, and sometimes they seem to take years. Often, a transformation has much to do with one's thoughts, perspectives, and frame of mind. Be patient as you take small steps in your spiritual growth. Taking time to breathe is a great start to any day, but it can be beneficial at any other time of day as well. Paying careful attention to this practice will help you systematically raise your vibration and energy—key ingredients in more easily connecting with your angels and guides.

Plan to set aside at least ten minutes of your time so you can fully engage in the exercise. Ideally, this exercise should be a great way to start your day. You can set your alarm ten to fifteen minutes earlier than normal, and then either sit up or lie in bed to perform the exercise. I prefer sitting up because I have been known to drift peacefully back to sleep if I remain lying down. If you think you will have the same problem, you can also find a good chair to sit in while you awaken your senses. Breathe a beautiful breath and commune with serenity.

The beauty of this exercise is the ease with which you can incorporate it into your life. Sprinkle the exercise into other parts of your day whenever you need a bit of clarity or an energy boost. You can find the time almost anywhere. However, to experience the full effectiveness and benefits, consider an environment that is mostly free of distractions. In a pinch, you can always sit in your car; facing a lovely park or lake is a great option, but at least try to face away from traffic if you can. The key is to respire in a tranquil place in order to achieve the best results.

> "Your visions will become clear only when you can
> look into your own heart. Who looks outside, dreams;
> who looks inside awakes."
> —Carl Jung

CHAPTER 2

Know Your Angels

A miracle is never lost. It may touch many people you
have never met, and produce undreamed of changes in
situations of which you are not even aware.

—*A Course in Miracles*

Heavenly angels always communicate through the high
vibration of love. Love is the most powerful emotion
on earth. The longer we are able to hold a positive thought
and emotion, the more powerful the energy of that emotion
becomes. Love is a necessary key ingredient to successfully
communicate with your loving angels and guides. Love
unites us to one another without qualifiers or judgment.
Love opens your heart to clear interaction with your angels
and to helping other people. Tapping into the power of love
and the human capacity to love are key to connecting with
your angels and guides. When engaged in the essence and
purity of heart, miracles happen. Everyone can communicate
with angels; all you need is an open mind, a desire to learn,
and a compassionate heart.

Angel–Decoding Secret Key #1
Love: express love, feel love, be loved,
know love, share love, reflect love, embrace love.

Defining *Angel*

Before we delve deeper into the process of angel decoding, let us define the term *angel* to help establish clarity, meaning, and understanding. When we hear the word *angel*, each of us may have our own definition. Although *angel* means "messenger," (Merriam-Webster) angels themselves—like the letters in our alphabet—appear to come in many forms, each with its own mystifying name. Typically, angels are considered celestial beings that are nonphysical in nature. Many references to angels occur in the Bible; for example, when Jesus speaks of twelve legions of angels in the book of Matthew. The Jewish Canon—specifically the Book of Enoch—references seven archangels. Medieval angelology mentions nine orders of angels. Each frame of history and nation appears to have its own niche in the angel world. For the purposes of this book, I will focus specifically on several powerful archangels, guardian angels, and our departed loved ones, also referred to by many as angels.

Guardian Angels

Each of us has been blessed with our own guardian angel. I believe God shared a moment with us before birth and said, "Here is a part of me to always be with you." These guardians then followed us into this world, promising to guide, protect, and encourage us on our life path. They are the essence of God's light—a state of grace in our world—and they tag along with us, waiting to be called upon. We are blessed with free will—a baffling concept that allows us to choose the direction of our life at any moment—and we often stumble through life, discovering what does or does not work for us and learning and growing along the way. Our guardian angels are bound by this decree, and they will not interfere with our freewill unless it is to guard us from the dangers of an untimely death. They take their job seriously, waiting patiently until we reach out in faith and ask for help. Pray to God, and ask your angels to help you in every area of your life, for they will do so with grace and gratitude.

Many people who have come to see me for individual spiritual readings ask me who their guardian angels are. Although we are each blessed with at least one guardian, there are many of us who have at least two or more. The number of angels around us at any given time is not finite and often represents a message being conveyed. I often refer to Doreen Virtue's book *Angel Numbers 101* for extended messages regarding the specific number of angels that present themselves around an individual during a session.

From a metaphysical perspective, the guardians are etheric energy—part of God's essence and love—and so being, they are egoless and do not have individual identities. The angels always want what is best for us, holding our highest interests at heart and supporting us with unconditional love and tenderness. No task is too difficult for them or too small. They are always with us and know our true purpose and direction in life. They work to support God's will in this world. An important aspect of God's will is the concept of peace, harmony, love, and joy. Our guardians put forth the highest good as a measure when granting our prayerful requests. Our growing faith and prayers amplify our desires and abilities to create goodwill and manifest miracles in our lives. Therefore, pray daily and often for the greatest good.

Guardian angels do not need names, yet they will tell you what to call them if you ask. They want to be as closely connected to you as possible, and they know that we humans connect names to one another as well as to the world around us. Asking for your guardian angel's name is a great start toward communicating with your angels.

Angel-Decoding Secret Key #2
Prayer, devotion, and meditation are the groundwork of success.

Asking for Your Guardian Angel's Name

Begin by returning to the centering-breath exercise from chapter 1. A state of relaxation, groundedness, and peaceful centeredness are very important to the process of receiving spiritual messages. You will find it easier to move into this relaxed state as you lend practice to this process. Once you have completed centering and are at peace with a quiet mind, begin saying a prayer, "Sweet Lord, beautiful angels, Holy Spirit, I ask that before this day is over, I come to know what to call my guardian angel. I am open to receiving and trust that it is for the highest good."

It is simple to ask; it is a bit harder to trust and allow the message to come to you. However, this is exactly what you will need to do. Relax, and go on about your day so you are truly giving the task to God and the angels and not forcing a response. The answer may show up in various forms and will often happen when you are vaguely occupied with something else. You may see a name that catches your eye, perhaps while reading an article or a book or maybe on a sign. The answer may appear in a dream or a sudden vision while you are daydreaming. You may hear a name in a song or a person nearby saying it, or it may come to you quietly in your subconscious. Your angel's name may be expressed through a feeling, a state of grace, love, or a gentle impression.

How the name of your guardian angel comes to you is the first lesson in how other messages will be revealed as you begin asking your angels for guidance more regularly. Your trust and patience is key to allowing your own spiritual gifts to be revealed to you. If you think you received an answer but are unsure or doubting, simply ask again. The angels love you very much and are willing to support you for as long as it takes. Please trust the process, and allow your angels to help you.

Departed Loved Ones

We also call loved ones who have crossed over angels. After a period of adjustment to their new existence in spirit, they check in on family members and friends still living on earth. Having been human, they have a recent understanding of the human condition and seem to connect more intimately with us in the way we would remember them. Their personalities seem to linger, presenting a likeness of who they once were. Still, as they are new to the spirit realm, they may not be the best source of guidance. Yet we miss them and want to know that they are happy—perhaps even joyous—and watching over us. Many times we find ourselves wondering if they are attuned to our current successes and challenges, if they are aware of how much we miss them, and if they have any messages for us.

Connecting with our departed loved ones is as easy as thinking of them. Actually, when a departed loved one comes to mind, it is most likely that they are, in that moment, nearby. Say hello, and feel their loving energy. Many people have vivid dreams in which they experience seeing and receiving a message from their loved ones. This type of dream is considered a genuine visitation. More information is covered in later chapters regarding our departed loved ones and the subtle messages they share with us to let us know they are well and in God's loving presence.

Spirit Guides

Spirit guides have lived on earth at one time or another, usually before your birth. Guides will meet with you before your incarnation and form a loving agreement to support your current life. You have chosen them because of their wisdom and the focus of your destiny for this life. They understand the human condition and have the responsibility of bringing balance to your life. Many guides have experienced the most difficult of human challenges: heartache, loss, betrayal, devastation, rejection, guilt, envy, greed, and grief. Due to the scope of their human experience, they are graced with wisdom and immeasurable compassion. Experience is a great teacher, and your spirit guides have the full curriculum.

Guides can also be very instrumental in supporting the structure of our lives and the creative energy that drives us. You can have and call on more than one guide, and there is no limit to the inspiration they can provide. Another of my mentors, Sonia Choquette, PhD, is especially fond of spirit guides. The author of *Ask Your Guides: Connecting to Your Divine Support System,* she suggests we call on guides for every category we can imagine: joy, organization, scheduling, advice, childrearing, marriage, medicine, healing, nature, art, music, and success, to name just a few, for the list is endless. Each of us has a support team from the higher realms, and we only need to hold an intention of what we need to have the support manifest.

Spirit guides—like angels and our deceased loved ones— are bound to the spiritual laws of free will, so they can help only if we request their assistance and allow them to support us in our lives. It is always safe and smart to call on the divine wisdom of the heavenly guides. Our divine helpers are provided by God to sustain and enrich our human experience.

Archangels

Each archangel oversees a specialized area of need. These beautiful beacons of light supervise our guardian angels, and they manage to cover the entire planet with their love. Archangels are capable of being in many places at once. They are not limited to time and space and can divide themselves among thousands of people in need of their specialty. Many books have been written describing the various archangels in great detail. One of my mentors, Doreen Virtue PhD, has written multiple books dedicated to the topic of angels, so you can find detailed information about the archangels, including the origin and history of each, in many of her books. My book is focused primarily on angel communication in general rather than specific angels and their specialties, but I will highlight three archangels whose areas of specialization are the ones we need most frequently.

My favorite archangel is Michael, the angel of power, strength, and protection. I often call on Michael and request that he is at my children's side when I feel they need protection or soulful strength. Michael is known to be tall, beautiful, and mighty. In Hebrew, *Michael* means "he who is like God," so we can assume that he is gorgeous, courageous, and loving. In accordance to the Roman Catholic Church, Archangel Michael is known also as Saint Michael, the patron saint of police officers. Many police officers wear Saint Michael medallions and intentionally touch them before going into potentially dangerous situations. An intention is a powerful call to the angels to support us in whatever way we may need. When you want to invoke Michael, simply state his name followed by your request, and the rest will be taken care of.

Archangel Raphael is the angel in charge of healing. According to the "Book of Tobit" contained in Catholic and Orthodox bibles, Raphael travels on a long journey with a young man, Tobias. On the journey Raphael uses protective healing powers, revealing his true identity at the end of the journey. (Tobit 12:15) His name means "God heals," Call on him to surround family and friends in need of healing light and love. Ask him to heal relationships, emotions, and physical ailments and to support any medical personnel who are working with you or your family in the healing process. He is known to have emerald-green energy that radiates healing light. When you pray, imagine this amazing color as a ray of healing energy, and it will amplify the intention to heal. Raphael is known to work very closely with Jesus, the great healer, teacher, counselor, and leader at the heart of the Christian church. To invoke Raphael, state his name followed by your request, and you will send good intentions and love to the person or situation in need of healing.

Archangel Gabriel is in charge of communication and the arts. His name means "strength of God." Gabriel is credited with bringing the message of the Christ birth to the Holy Mother Mary, and so he is also credited with the important job of selecting souls to be born into the material world. He works closely with parents who are praying for a new birth in their families. (Archangels and Ascended Masters, Virtue) Gabriel's work is dear to my heart, as I view communication as the key to good relationships and the key for those of us who are teachers and authors with a message to share, imbue, and inspire. I often feel his gentle presence when I am writing or speaking. The focus of this book is communication, and therefore, Gabriel's influence has had an immense impact throughout my writing process. Gabriel supports positive conversations and a powerful mind-set of community. He brings with him the essence of collaboration, which is so very important in our world if we are to live joyfully—we must acknowledge the fact that we are all connected. To invoke Gabriel, state his name followed by your request, and be confident that miracles do happen. Please take a moment now to ask Gabriel to support your efforts in communicating with the angels. Your success will follow.

Tips to Support You on Your Angel-Decoding Journey

Love is a key ingredient to success as you open your heart to communication with your angels and guides.

Prayer and centering is essential groundwork to receiving messages from the divine, whether from your guardian angels, the archangels, spirit guides, or departed loved ones.

Invoke your angels, the archangels, and guides by holding a clear intention of your desire for the greatest good of those in need, including yourself.

Think of your departed loved one and he/she will be there beside you in spirit—often before your thought is complete.

Chapter 3

Hear Your Angels

Seek first to understand, then to be understood.
—Stephen R. Covey

When I first arrived in the United States at the age of six, I knew only a few words of English. In order to understand what people were saying, I listened carefully to the words they spoke, but I also focused on social and verbal communication cues. Even when I didn't fully understand the words being spoken, I found I could discern the main points of a conversation by paying attention to what was communicated through gestures, facial expressions, emotions, energy, and vibration. Isn't this how we all learn to communicate? As young babies, we intuited the grander aspects of speech without needing to grasp the exact meaning of each individual word. As young children, we learned to pick up on vocal tone, rate, and inflection to aid our interpretation of what had been said, and this knowledge often helped us gauge where we stood with our parents and teachers.

Learning to speak in our native tongue was easy due to language immersion. We heard people speaking all the time. We may have encountered language through the radio or television every day. We saw the written word and associated these symbols with mental images as our ears tuned into the sounds and we made connections.

Neural pathways within the brain forge the sounds and patterns of our literary experiences. Research and science prove that language pathways begin to become hardwired in the brain at the approximate age of seven. This is also about the time when children enter what educational psychologist Jean Piaget deemed "The Age of Logic" in his theory of intellectual development.

I am an average individual. However, I count my blessings every day for my pronounced intuitive and psychic abilities. To my understanding, the science behind why I am blessed with these gifts appears to coincide with the theory of cognitive development and language acquisition. Around seven, the typical child is naturally shifting to greater use of his or her logical, analytical, left-brain abilities. This is when most children begin to question the validity of Santa Claus and the Tooth Fairy. It is the age when children begin to apply analysis and discern more logically. As brain development continues, there is a tendency to ignore the subtle innuendos of emotion while placing more focus on concrete matter, logic, and reasoning.

Remember: there are no accidents. The universe synchronistically orchestrated my arrival in America to coincide with a time just prior to my seventh birthday. I was suddenly immersed in a new culture and unable to speak the language, so I used intuition to understand what people were saying or implying. So at a time when most children are beginning to shift into their logical, analytical frame of mind, I had the opportunity to focus and practice instead on the use of my intuitive, expressive, right-brain abilities. These abilities include creativity, intuition, emotional expression and comprehension, and artistic acuity.

I share this information simply because I have often been asked, "Why you, Maria? Why do you have this intuitive gift?" The answer is simple: I had a wonderful mentor—my grandmother—who taught me to trust in God, my angels, and my soul. Beyond that, I guess you could say I was in the right place at the right time.

The circumstances of your own life have brought you to this book. You were guided here to improve your chances of learning a new skill while also learning a bit more about angels. There are no accidents; the timing is perfect for you. You are ready to enhance your intuitive abilities, for the brain is an amazingly pliable organ. All you have to do is begin right now making better use of your right brain, for neurogenesis—the brain's ability to forge new pathways—occurs throughout life.

In chapter 1, we covered centered breathing and how to incorporate this relaxing and rejuvenating practice into your daily routine. I cannot emphasize the practice enough. Every time I need to ask angels for guidance, I first go to the centered space where I am calm and my soul is open to the power of the Holy Spirit. The centering-breath exercise is where you activate your intuitive mind. You are also encouraged to begin paying closer attention to the innuendos and sensations of this world and the unlimited context of the mystical world, for you are just inches away from full activation of your intuitive potential. You will naturally begin noticing subtle impressions that never before seemed important. You will come to appreciate the complexities of your inner guidance and the simplicity of accessing the holiness and guidance of your soul.

We know cavemen did not read books as we do today. Who is to say that angel decoding is not the way of the future? Every means of communication has changed in the last few decades. We used to have telephones attached to the walls of our homes, and now we walk around with handheld computers, smartphones, and tablets while communicating through cyberspace, social networks, and instant messaging. Messages travel from one device to the other as signals sent through towers. In the case of angel decoding, you are the device and God is the tower. Tap into your potential for inspiration, for there are no accidents and no limits to your capacity for creation as scientific discoveries and new inventions abound.

Current scientific research involving the heart and brain has documented specific ways of activating and engaging your orbital cortex, a part of the brain critical for emotional awareness and its effect on regulating decision making. One method of activation is to calm the mind, such as we do in meditative and contemplative practices. Especially interesting are studies completed by the George Lucas Educational Foundation involving emotional and learning capacities. It was noted that "positive" emotions, such as patience, calmness, and love, directly support the brain's ability to learn and greatly increase successful outcomes in learning new skills. "Negative" emotions, such as anger, frustration, and depression, interfere with learning and brain development. This evidence is an argument for creating safe, calm, and caring relationships in all avenues of our culture, but especially where learning takes place. Even more obvious is the relevance that positive emotions have in the successful application of learning strategies for intuitive practice. Love, joy, happiness, and a tranquil mind will support your successful spiritual journey as an angel decoder.

The teacher in me is excited about the prospect of your success. What matters most is your desire for spiritual growth and alignment with your authentic nature. We are all wired for intuition, so bring awareness to your intuitive channels and potential skills. Progressive intuitive growth will take time and practice. As you honor yourself and discover a closer relationship with God and the angels, the more rewarding your life will become. As you embrace your true nature and engage your heart more fully into spiritual growth, the more defined your path in life will become. You can transform yourself and be an exemplar of change toward a brighter life for yourself and for others.

Taking care of the body, mind, and spirit is an important component of improving your life and your potential as a successful, insightful, vibrant, and joyful human being. As corporal beings, we need our bodies to sustain us as we engage deliberately on our spiritual paths.

Tips for Renewing Your Soul

Quiet your mind by engaging in centered breathing for ten to fifteen minutes every day as outlined in chapter 1.

- ☐ Make time to fill your soul with love by developing healthy, loving relationships.
- ☐ Fill your body with vibrant, fresh foods that are as close to natural as possible.
- ☐ Make time to play, and exercise your body and heart for thirty minutes a day.
- ☐ Drink plenty of pure water to hydrate your mind and body.
- ☐ Sleep at least seven to nine hours every night.
- ☐ Pray to God, and ask your angels to help you and guide you often.

Chapter 4

I Heard the Angels Speak

If trouble hearing angels' song with thine ears, try listening with thy heart.

—Terri Guillemets

Your own pronounced intuition is just a tune-up away. If you are ready, it is time to embark on the real essence of angel decoding and begin to converse with your loving angels and guides. There are various empathic sensory systems and terms to define and highlight. In the coming chapters, we will dive into each of these ideas more deeply, sharing important keys and guidelines toward your successful angel-decoding adventure.

The most prominent of the intuitive gifts are clairaudience, claircognizance, clairvoyance, and clairsentience—or to describe each more directly: clear hearing, knowing, seeing, and feeling.

We will now begin the practical steps of divine guidance.

Angel-Decoding Secret Key #3
Learning to read the messages of divine consciousness
requires good learning habits and practice.

Clairaudience ~ Clear Hearing

Clairaudience—also known as clear hearing—is the ability to pick up on or tune into a higher vibrational frequency by sensing it through the auditory channels. We can liken it to having supersonic hearing. When we first experience language, it occurs naturally through the triangular area that encompasses the ears, nose, and throat. This experience of resonance is natural to us. Most of us take our sense of hearing for granted, and therefore, we fail to appreciate the greater breadth of our abilities.

The deaf have a more pronounced sense of the vibrational experience of sound. I am reminded of a scene from the 1986 movie *Children of a Lesser God*. The speech teacher has his deaf students sitting on a stereo with the music blasting to the ends of the campus so they can experience the vibration of the music. The students are deaf, but they are clearly enjoying the encounter. Some are drumming to the beat, and others are sensing the lively experience through their derrieres.

Sound is the vibration of air molecules traveling from one location to another. Your eardrum picks up on the molecular movement using tiny auditory instruments, and then the vibrations are sent to your brain as messages to be interpreted.

It is possible to have varying degrees of hearing abilities. And it is possible to develop your ability to recognize various types of sound, even the subtlest vibrations, in order to better communicate with your angels. Your angels and guides would love to help you with this process, so begin by asking them to support your efforts to hear their loving messages more clearly. Then relax and trust the process, for it is when we are calm, centered, and open to love that we can hear, know, feel, and see our heavenly support system.

Love for yourself and others is a key ingredient in any spiritual development. We cannot intimately connect with the higher resources of heaven without compassionately loving others and ourselves. The ability to love is a powerful catalyst toward opening your intuitive channels.

Clairaudience—clear mystical hearing—opens with your request. Ask God to help you hear his voice, and ask your angels to express their loving presence so you can experience their vibrations. A simple prayerful request can lead the way: "Beautiful Lord and angels, I ask that you remove any blocks or fears which are preventing me from hearing your loving messages. I ask that I can clearly hear heaven's messages and the beautiful song of your voice speaking to my soul. This or better God."

It was 1994 when I first heard my guardian angel state his name. Earlier in the day, I had been reading a book about angels, and the author had suggested that if we ask our guardian angel for a name to call him or her, we would receive an answer. I had nothing to lose in trying, so I said a silent prayer to God and then asked my guardian angel to reveal a name to me before the day was over. Afterward, I went about my day as usual and let the angels take care of granting my request.

Later in the evening, as I read a storybook to my young daughter, I was taken aback when I heard a unique name clearly present itself in my mind. It was as if someone had whispered this name directly within my brain and separately from my reading experience. My thinking mind was focused on the book and the process of reading aloud. It is hard to describe the sensation of the message, but I clearly heard the name Marucio.

Immediately, I recalled that I had asked—or rather, I had prayed—to know what to call my guardian angel, and now here was the answer. I had asked God in faith, released the "how" to the angels, and opened myself to the miracle of their work. After this profound experience, I promptly thanked God and the angels and continued to finish the book I was reading to my sweet child.

Later that night, I wrote of the experience in my journal, thrilled to have completed the first of many teachings from my wonderful angels. Up until that day, I had shut down many of my early intuitive teachings from Vovo. I guess I had been busy attending to conventional life: completing school; attaining first a bachelors degree and then a masters in education; finding my soul mate and getting married; discovering my first, second, and third careers; and having my first and then second child. I had been stumbling through the typical experiences of life with my eyes half open and my heart hopeful. I had God and prayers but not the empirical relationship with God that I now have come to understand as the true vehicle of my spiritual awareness and the song of my soul. My angels have been by my side all along, prompting and encouraging me back to the true essence of my soul. However, for many years, I was not paying attention.

In Divine Time . . . We Awaken

After my arrival in America at the age of six, I set about becoming an American. I wanted the "American dream" and all the freedom and abundance that it implies. In my first year, I learned to speak English and became deeply infused in the culture. I shifted quickly into being a typical American kid. As Vovo had taught me, I continued praying every day and night—and often in between—but I didn't need to engage all my extra senses, so I innocently neglected my old friends, the angels. I was busy, and America is full of sumptuous distractions, so these things moved me more than just physically away from the quiet and somewhat isolated life I had lived in Brazil with my grandmother and aunt. I had my mother and a new life. I was safe and sound in America, my new home.

I recall occasionally using the heart-to-heart connection technique (mentioned in the introduction) to check in with my Vovo back in Brazil. When I checked in with her energy and heart, she always felt warm and loving but also a little tired and sad. I didn't like to dwell there because it made me feel tired and sad too. So instead, I prayed for her and my family in Brazil and focused on growing up. That way, I could make enough money to someday bring Vovo to America to live with us. I knew she was proud to hear of my successes, that I was doing well in school, had lots of friends, and was participating in many school activities. She was happy for me and the strides I had made, for I had accomplished more than she had ever dreamed for me. Yet she was so very far away and removed from my new life. My mother and I sent her photos and called to talk over the phone during the holidays, but I never saw her again.

Vovo was my first spiritual mentor, a master of love and endearment, and a solid example of maternal presence. She was truly a steadfast soldier of grace in this world. She lived until my twenty-first birthday and then died in the spring of that same year. When I learned of her death, I cried until I felt her presence, an experience I can describe only as a warm embrace. I felt a definite shift in the energy surrounding me, a familiarity that touched the core of my soul, for my spirit seemed to sing with the love I had come to associate with her presence. In my mind today, Vovo is still by me, and I feel her gentle presence, see her shy, toothless grin, and know she loves me eternally.

Which brings me to my first clairaudient connection with my guardian angel. It came approximately twelve years after the death of my grandmother, which seems like such a large gap in time. But I share this truth to reveal and lend credence to the adage that we must truly desire and be open to our individual spiritual gifts before the awareness and the remembrance of our gifts can be slowly and gently revealed to us. Except for experiencing a spiritual hug from Vovo when she died, I had stopped paying attention to my angels from the time I was seven years old until I was well into my thirties. For those twenty-some years of human life, the angels never left my side; they were and still are always with me. However, once I was enlightened to their presence again, the lessons and support in communicating with them came flooding back to me as familiar as an old, trusted friend.

Specifics Regarding Clairaudience

Clairaudient messages come in various forms. The first step is to pray by asking your angels for clarity or for an answer to a problem or question. Then you need to be open to receiving answers in any form they may appear. Your ability to let go of the outcome and trust what you receive is important. If you are feeling tense or anxious, you can miss the answer.

One method of receiving a message is to hear it within your mind like a whisper or a thought that appears separate from any other thoughts or mental activities. At first, it is typical for the answer to come to you when you are focused on activities that are more automatic, such as driving, washing dishes, reading, daydreaming, or playing. You hear or intuit the communication while your mind is occupied by something else.

A message can also appear in the form of a song playing on the radio, a phrase embedded in a text, or something said by a television character. A person in your life may even state the message at a time when you need to hear those exact words. You may be familiar with the expression, "I heard the call." Angels will bring messages to you in any way that will make sense to you.

If you are feeling unsure about a message you think you may have received, it is perfectly acceptable to ask for clarity. Angels are consistent, positive, and patient. If my angels waited years for me to pay attention, yours will be just as accommodating. Trust what you receive as messages and then begin recognizing how you are most often receiving the communications and when they have the most clarity. Your angels are teaching you their lexicon, and you will begin to build your own unique glossary of impressions, symbols, words, and numbers.

When doing readings for others, I always pray before the session. Then I take several deep breaths, and within the clear, calm environment of my office, miracles happen. Oftentimes, the messages are so clear I hear exact phrases and names. My clients are often amazed at how these phrases sound just as if their loved ones had spoken them, and pertinent names frequently appear just when they are needed. I have used this same process thousands of times, asking any number of questions over the years, so please don't expect to be an overnight angel-decoding expert right away. Your ability to understand the messages will take time, just as learning to read involved an understanding of one step that would then unveil the next step needed on the way to mastering comprehension. First, you learned letters and then sounds, followed by words and, finally, sentences. Angel decoding will take a similar path of practice and application.

As my level of trust and intuitive awareness has developed, the time frame for getting a response has compressed. Just like any other skill, practice has made the process smoother and more immediate. When I first started expanding my intuitive abilities, I would include time qualifiers in my prayer requests, such as "before this day is over" or "by the end of the week." I did this because answers to my requests were not always timely. Not to imply that the angels were slow to respond, but rather that I may have missed the answers due to my lack of experience. The angels have taught me to recognize the various symbols and subtle impressions, and, in essence, they have taught me to decode—or read—their language. As of this writing, I can ask my angels a question and often the answer arrives before I finish the sentence.

The more occasions I have had to spend time in a prayerful mind-set, the more defined this form of decoding has and continues to become. I must emphasize again the value of centering and calming yourself and the importance of a contemplative environment to support your receptive awareness. It is also a good idea to begin a journal or glossary of words, images, impressions, or symbols that are showing up for you as you work through the angel-decoding process.

Tips for Receiving Clairaudient Messages:

- ☐ Be in a center of prayerfulness, love, and peace.
- ☐ Find a calm environment away from distractions.
- ☐ Ask questions with clarity and good intentions. Angels will bring guidance and loving cautions, never messages of doom.
- ☐ Ask questions pertaining to the highest good of all concerned.
- ☐ Keep questions simple.
- ☐ Questions related to the future will have answers based on probability, and they should be considered as such.

A Miracle Message from Maverick

I have been an angel-therapy practitioner and spiritual medium for well over twelve years. Thousands of readings and sessions with clients have helped me gradually improve my skills and gifts as an intuitive. In all that time, I have never audibly heard a message from an animal. I have connected with many departed pets, usually through feelings and by knowing their presence and sensing their love as it radiates energy, personality, and charm. But recently, something different occurred: I *heard* a message from a special pet belonging to a client named Pamela.

The session started just like any other, with a prayer and special messages from Pamela's guardian angels. Then, as I looked into Pamela eyes before asking her what questions she had for the angels, I heard, "Mav." I wasn't sure if I heard correctly, so I asked Pamela, "Do you know a Max?" She said, "Do you mean Mav?" And of course I said, "Yes!" Then I asked, "Is Mav a dog?" She started to cry and nodded her head. Maverick Joe, her beloved dog, had died recently, and he wanted to be sure she knew he was well and, apparently, was now *talking*.

Our pets are amazing companions in life. Their love for us transcends time through space and into eternity. They, too, are safe in heaven, where all great souls unite and where we will all meet again. Love has no end and extends beyond the limits of mind, species, and self-imposed segregation.

Questions about the Future

Sometimes you just can't wait until tomorrow to know how a situation will turn out. It is absolutely fine to ask your angels and guides about future outcomes. However, since every moment is being created out of the accumulation of previous moments, outcomes cannot be set in stone. Answers dealing with the future are based on probability. A future situation can be read in the present moment using your present state of being. If your state of being changes only slightly, the predicted results or outcome will be more likely. If you change dramatically, however, so will your outcome.

Here is an example: You ask your angels if you are going to get a new job before the year is over. The angels may reply with a strong "Yes" or "Affirmative." Or you might hear,

"It is most probable." Since we are all blessed with free will, you can decide to steer your life in any direction you choose. So as you exercise your free will, here are some potential directions you might choose:

1. You can live basically as you have been living.
2. You can decide to become a full-time drug addict.
3. You can buy a winning lotto ticket.

You get the picture. As long as you continue to lead your life in the same manner you enjoyed previously, your reading of the future should maintain. Any of the other choices you engage in because of your free will can and will dictate a different outcome.

It is usually easier to ask and receive answers for other people if you do not know them intimately. Our objectivity can become clouded by the emotional connections we have with another individual. That being said, I have found that going back into a center of clarity or pure intention is often the best formula for clear and loving answers, no matter the question. So start applying your clairaudient abilities today! Let's look at how you can do it.

First, for what in your life would you like to have more clarity? Hold the intention (the question) in your mind, and then release it to the angels. Remember, it is important to stop trying to control the answer or the outcome. Establish a gentle time frame as well, such as before today is over or by tomorrow.

Here is a quick, step-by-step description of how to ask your angels for guidance:

- ☐ Take a deep, clearing breath.
- ☐ Ask your question clearly, simply, and lovingly (and include a time frame if you wish).
- ☐ Let go of the outcome and the means by which an answer will come.
- ☐ Your answer can come in many forms and at any time (we will discuss more methods of connecting in the coming chapters).
- ☐ Be open and relaxed, and be sure to take notes about the experience in a notebook, journal, or glossary containing related angel messages.

Fine-Tuning Your Clairaudience

Your experience may begin by clairaudiently receiving single-word answers. Then it may build to short phrases, complete sentences, and eventually bloom into whole conversations. Work at increasing your personal vibration by filling your life with joy, playfulness, prayerfulness, and peace. Consider calling on the angels to help clear your ear chakras. You can also schedule an appointment with an energy healer or Reiki practitioner to specifically aid you in removing any negative energy or emotional blocks from your system and to support fine-tuning your intuitive energies. Remember the importance of taking good care of your health in order to improve your ability to hear spirit more clearly. Angel decoding requires daily practice and direct application; practice by asking your angels questions regarding any area of your life. Listen and apply the guidance you receive, and you will find your skills improving quickly. More importantly, your life journey will begin to open to greater abundance and joy. You are learning an amazing skill—put it into practice! With persistence, your abilities will naturally increase. And really, what do you have to lose? Nothing! Embrace the opportunity to converse with the divine.

The answers from your angels are always

- □ good for God,
- □ good for others, and
- □ good for you.

Affirm daily: "I hear my angels speaking clearly to my heart and mind. I am clairaudient!"

CHAPTER 5

Born Knowing

The only real valuable thing is intuition.
—Albert Einstein

Sometimes we just know what we know, without understanding how the knowledge came to be. Claircognizance is when clear, mystical thinking aligns with inspired knowing. Apparently, when Einstein was working on an idea and felt stuck, he would either take a nap or go to bed for the night. Upon waking, the answer to his puzzle or a new idea about it was often suddenly clear to him. It was as if a brainstorm of inspiration and understanding was unlocked during his rest and a new awareness became available to him. He wisely credited this onset of knowledge to intuition.

Angel-Decoding Secret Key #4
Faith is to believe and to know truth without understanding how you know.

41

Claircognizance ~ Clear Knowing

Claircognizance—or clear knowing—is the ability to understand certain things without directly being told. Information is downloaded into the mind via thought, insight, or inspiration. This intuitive information may present itself as a comprehensive understanding of something, or other times, it may appear as small bits of information or subtle insights into the thinking mind. Often, people who are more left-brained, or analytical, have a stronger sense of claircognizance. These people with a heightened sense of clear knowing are commonly dubbed "know-it-alls."

Being aware of your claircognizance and applying your gift to support your life and the lives of others is a tricky task. Often, this ability is dismissed as an overactive imagination, and all the amazing potential—for inventions, solutions, cures, art—is overlooked because the person receiving the knowledge never put it to use. Value your understanding and mystical "knowings." Of all the intuitive abilities, claircognizance is not as well known, but despite its subtler nature, it is just as powerful as the others. Clear knowing often shows up synchronistically during an ordinary day in your life. Making good use of a synchronistic experience can—and usually does—bring future success.

Recently, I had an opportunity to view a segment of TedTV in which an eleven-year-old boy with autism was presenting. The title of his presentation was "Forget Everything You Know." According to this young man, he had been pulled out of his regular classroom because his teachers said he couldn't learn. While segregated from his classmates and sitting idly, he started focusing on the ideas, interests, impressions, and understandings that he was capable of in the subject that he was most interested in: mathematics. He shared with the audience that he was currently working on publishing a mathematical theorem. He claimed it was when he stopped trying to think that the solutions to mathematical problems began to reveal themselves. And it all happened synchronistically with the event of his teachers placing him outside of his regular classroom.

While others misunderstood his distinctive learning style, this young man found an opportunity to quietly discover for himself his underlying brilliance. This is an excellent example of a person making good use of a synchronistic experience. We don't all think, process, or approach comprehension in equal ways. Nevertheless, we have surprising capabilities when we give credence to our uniqueness and recognize our key gifts. Embrace what you know to be true for you, and do not let rejection or fear keep you from your greatest potential and desires.

Thank goodness this young man was allowed to audit a few college-level math classes because today he is an associate math professor at a university and will soon publish his first mathematical theorem—at the ripe old age of eleven!

Automatic Writing ~ A Form of Channeling

As I write this chapter, I ask my angels and guides to work with me and through me to bring forth its content. Writers are often claircognizant. The process lends itself to moments of genuine inspiration. I often feel I am taking divine dictation rather than needing to think about what I write. The process is similar to a concept referred to as automatic writing.

Automatic writing is an effective tool for engaging your subconscious to open up and effectively use claircognizance. So grab a pen, pencil, crayon, or keyboard, and simply start writing or drawing to your heart's content. Do not judge what comes through. Instead, love yourself, your work, and your revelations. Have fun reflecting on the mysteries of what appears. Reviewing your ramblings can reveal new ideas ready for you to explore. Clarity and direction are other benefits of this process.

Faith is believing without knowing why you believe. Have faith because true claircognizance will inspire you to help and serve others while improving your life at the same time. Clear, mystical knowing doesn't need explanation; it will simply be true, good, and pure.

Tips for Receiving Clear Claircognizance

- ☐ Call upon your angels and guides to shift your vibration into a high state of love.
- ☐ Spend time in quiet meditation (guided or self-directed).
- ☐ Embrace faith, and trust your knowings.
- ☐ True claircognizant messages will be good for you, good for others, and good for God.

- Claircognizance comes from wisdom, never control or power.
- Doodle, write, diagram, or jot down ideas and inspirations. Usually, they will appear step-by-step; as you finish one piece or part, the next is revealed.
- When you know, you know. So get out of your ego, and lovingly share your insight. It is meant to improve your life and the lives of others—so share!
- Give value to your truly inspired ideas.

Examples of Claircognizance

- You awaken from a dream with the exact answer you have been seeking.
- You are introduced to a new person and seem to know details about them without knowing how.
- After meditation, you know just how to approach an issue with which you have been struggling.
- A nagging, enlightening impression keeps coming into your awareness.
- While exercising, doing yoga, or running, an inspirational idea prompts you to action.
- You know someone is lying despite contradicting evidence.
- You spontaneously blurt out an answer to a question or comment—and you are right! Often, a blurt can be embarrassing, as it is a comment everyone else was thinking but no one would speak aloud.
- You appear to know or have a strong premonition of events to come.

- ☐ Information seems to come from nowhere, and it has nothing to do with what you were thinking about or doing.

Premonitions ~ A Claircognizant Reality

Premonitions are future related. It is important to remember that future-related images and ideas are based on probability, not inevitability. Angels and guides do not ever present information or revelations in an alarming manner. Instead, they are presented as cautions. When you receive a cautionary premonition that does seem disturbing, it is usually a call for prayer. Prayer is a powerful and affirming way to manifest a positive resolution for all concerned. Prayer is an important strategy.

No doubt many of us working in the "light" may be called on to pray for the best future outcome. Turn worries into powerful, life-lifting prayers. We can easily shift into the prayer frequency and increase our capacity to bring love and balance to a person, place, or event.

Challenges may come our way, but with prayer, we can shift them toward the best possible outcome. With prayer, we can project protection and relief and send support and strength. The benefits of prayer have been proven, even when the praying is done unawares.

Worry does nothing. Cross out and cancel your worries by saying a prayer for the better. Pray for the outcomes you wish to see in the world. Prayer is time-tested, pure, unselfish, and loving.

How to Ward Off a Potential Disaster

A few years ago, my parents were planning a trip out of the country. I woke with a start one morning prior to their departure, feeling concerned about a dream I had just had. In the dream, I saw an airplane in flight with luggage and other debris falling from the sky. My first reaction was to call my parents and ask how their plans were going for the trip. I did not tell them about my dream; I just reviewed their plans with them. We ended the call by stating our love for one another and the comment, "Safe travels. Go with God."

Upon hanging up the phone, I took a few minutes to center myself, and in a prayerful state, I asked Archangel Michael— the angel of courage, strength, and protection—to support my parents on their trip to Brazil. I prayed they would arrive safely, have a grand and wonderful trip, and then return home safely. I imagined the smiles and how love-filled their souls would be as they reconnected with family.

Affirm: "All is well"

My parents did have a wonderful trip, and they did return home safely. The only glitch was that their luggage was lost for several days when they first arrived in Brazil. It was a great reminder that all is not always as it seems, and it confirmed the power of prayer as a spiritual, loving tool. It was also an important example of using discernment to establish what is truthful and within your capacity to honestly direct through prayer.

In my dream, I saw the luggage flying from the plane, and so it was, in its way, a true premonition. However, my interpretation of the dream caused me unwarranted fear. I understood that, instead of alarming others, I needed to project a positive intention, a prayer for those concerned. As a result, the outcome reflected the intention of the prayer for the highest good of all.

Remember to pray when you have a worry; the power of prayer can bless your life and the lives of others.

Affirm daily: "My angels graciously share with me clear, understandable information and brilliant moments of divine inspiration. I am claircognizant!"

CHAPTER 6

Vibration at the Rate of Love

Angel-Decoding Secret Key #5
It's not about you! Angel communication is about
embracing purpose and seeing the grander
vision of your mission as a soul.

Angels Help with Relationships

Many of my clients value their personal relationships above all other aspects of their lives. But oftentimes, our close relationships can be strained by the greater responsibilities of life. Spouses, children, parents, and close friends often require the best of us but may end up seeing the worst. When you find yourself in a quandary of how to handle a particular situation involving a personal relationship, asking angels for help can bring healing insight and support.

When I asked angels for guidance with my own marital struggles, I started receiving deeper understanding regarding my spouse's feelings, personal challenges, and frame of mind.

Divine claircognizance was immediate and clear when I lovingly opened my heart. Angels confirmed that my spouse loved me and that his current disconcerting state and emotional distance had very little to do with our relationship and much more to do with his frustration at work.

I was guided to be more sympathetic to his plight as he worked through this brief challenge. Patiently, I prompted him to relax while at home and feel free to share or vent his concerns. I reminded him that I was the friend he married, and I would not judge him. Rather, I wanted him to feel comfortable sharing his struggles with me.

Eventually, he revealed his concerns along with confiding that he kept all his frustrations to himself because he didn't want me to worry. But he didn't realize that he had become despondent and argumentative. He thought he was protecting me by keeping his work issues to himself. At first, I thought that perhaps I was the problem, but I came to find that his distress had nothing to do with me at all. This is so often the case for many of our relationship issues.

Of course, the angels were right. When I looked outside myself and called on heavenly direction, faith revealed the truth, and I took action by trusting what I clearly knew was good for me, good for others, and good with God.

Nothing is ever as it seems. There are so many times when spirit has rescued me and my loved ones by presenting various points of view. Many clients have expressed similar experiences when calling on the angels for help. Focusing on increasing your energy to the vibration of love will move you out of ego-based stubbornness and self-centeredness and move you forward instead. Here again, love can heal a broken heart or a crippled relationship.

Remember, when practicing to improve intuition, you need to trust and embrace what you naturally know. Help is always available when you open your heart and faith to God and the angels. Angelic assistance always manifests in the form of truthful loving messages. Love forgives, cures, embraces, understands, shares, cuddles, supports, balances, heals, provides, and connects. In all of existence, only love is real.

My work as a professional angel therapist and intuitive life coach is very rewarding. Daily, I have the opportunity to work with a variety of clients who are drawn to my work. In private sessions, I have witnessed miraculous moments of healing where a client's perceptions realign with their truth and positive outcomes are the result. Many times, a heavenly message is just what they needed to hear. Grateful clients thank me, and I am always gracious, but I give all glory to God and his angels. I am the middle person, the guide and teacher working to support a channel for God's light to shine on each person. The messages and sessions are not about me; I am the go-between, and I understand the grander work at hand. I am a teacher of teachers, and I look forward to supporting those who are ready to embark on their spiritual journey.

I anticipate the day when more people are systematically knowledgeable about the sophisticated concepts of chakras, auras, and energy fields; a day when suggesting that someone "check in" doesn't lead them to reach for their cell phone, but rather they close their eyes, breathe deeply, and call on their loving angels. I imagine a time when I say, "I do angel readings," and the person sitting next to me responds with "So do I!"

We are truly spiritual beings having a human experience. Try to recall who *you* really are. We are connected to one another in a unified energy vortex. This force field grows stronger with the vibration of love, expanding with our good intentions. Your ability to think positively about yourself and others can charge the field exponentially with unprecedented results. Be the force you want to see in this world. Travel at the speed of love.

Heighten Your Intuitive Abilities with the Vibration of Love

The highest frequency known to man is the state of love. Your ability to decode or discern between ordinary information and extraordinary information is linked to your vibrational state. When I speak of love as a frequency, I am referring to unconditional love—a selfless, giving, all-accepting love.

As we develop from babies to adults, we experience love at many levels. At first, when we are infants, we demand attention to our needs and are often incapable of returning love to those who tend to us. As we grow, we begin to barter for love. We may share our toys or snacks or warmly give a hug and a kiss in exchange for love. It isn't until we reach a point where we are caring for another person—or even a pet—that we offer unconditional love. At this stage, we are no longer bartering; we are giving unselfishly, and we have become a channel of love, serving others and focusing on their well-being and care.

In a state of unconditional love, we see the world around us with very different eyes. We feel expanded and full of peaceful, loving energy. We are joyful, peaceful, and secure. Many of us feel this way around our children, family, or close friends. The frequency of unconditional love is comfortable and never judgmental. It is an ingredient required for spiritual growth and communication.

If you want to improve your spiritual awareness, you must embrace the highest possible quality and degree of compassion. The highest vibration and frequency of love is synonymous with individuals who unselfishly and compassionately embody the ideals of attaining a greater good for all humanity. Pope John Paul II experienced an assassination attempt in 1981 and later openly forgave his would-be assassin, publicly hugging and embracing him. "Pray for my brother" was his plea.

Pope John Paul II may have experienced physical pain from the attempted assassination; however, his personal peace of mind and soul were undisturbed due to his ability to see the miracle in the holy moment and seize an opportunity to choose forgiveness. Christ-consciousness is an example to follow in striving for a focused embodiment and presence of the Holy Spirit among men. Your intuition and connection with your angels and guides will increase exponentially as your heart encompasses greater compassion for yourself and others.

Self-awareness is important to spiritual growth. Where you are emotionally will dictate what level of support and spiritual guidance you can receive, as well as how much you can provide for others. Practice checking in with yourself when you are frustrated or feeling unloved to see where your behaviors and expectations fall on the love barometer. You may find that a shift in your heart and attitude can help you heal from emotional pain and allow you to open yourself to greater understanding of what you truly need in any given situation. Being comfortable in your own skin becomes easier when you learn to laugh at yourself for acting out a "baby love" tantrum. You will grow spiritually and intuitively if you leave demanding and self-centered expectations out of your life and move into a mind-set of compassion and peace. Flip your internal emotional switch, and choose to find a happy compromise within yourself, as well as among those you love and care for. Answers, guidance, and support are always just a prayer away.

Angel–Decoding Secret Key #6
Heavenly angels always communicate through the high vibration of love. They want all the glory to go to God, and they are themselves a gift from God.

CHAPTER 7

Emotional Intelligence

Follow your heart and intuition. They already know what
you truly want to become. Everything else is secondary.
—Steve Jobs

M y grandmother was an amazing storyteller. She
could create a meal from scraps. She ruled by an
undemanding moral code. And she raised me with a firm,
loving devotion.

By the time I was born, Vovo had lost most of her teeth, and
she housed a stout, sturdy frame. Her long, black-and-silver-
streaked hair was worn in a single braid down her back, and
her deep, caramel eyes complemented her warm, bronze
skin. To me, Vovo was a fairy godmother. She always knew
what I needed, and she graced our simple life with the best
she could offer: her time, her stories, her hugs, a warm dish
of *feijao* (rice and beans, Brazilian-style), and weekly field
trips to the local open market.

To this day, I often feel my grandmother's presence nearby. When I was very young, Vovo taught me how to check in with my mother living five thousand miles away. She shared with me the power of the heart-to-heart connection. She showed me the way to clearly intuit, or feel, the essence of a person, place, or situation. She nudged me toward trusting my greater feelings and impressions. And she affirmed these practices by encouraging me to connect with my mother through the feelings of my heart when I missed her the most—and that happened multiple times a day for several years while we were apart.

Angel-Decoding Secret Key #7
Answers to your prayers begin with patience, trust, and faith, as prayerful devotion will grant clarity to the answers.

Clairsentience ~ Clear Feeling/Clear Sensing

A very prominent type of intuition is clairsentience, also known as the ability to sense and feel the emotions and energies of other people, objects, or places. Through physical sensations, vibrations, and presence, you can perceive the physical experiences and intentions of people in the room with you or even those living in a distant location. People with pronounced clairsentient abilities can transcend margins of species, sustaining communication with pets, plants, crystals, and spirit.

In the early 1960s, Sao Paulo, Brazil, was often a bustling place, with thriving outdoor markets in various neighborhoods throughout the city. Local farmers would bring fresh produce and an eclectic selection of handmade crafts and wares to the markets. From the high-rise apartment where I lived with Vovo and my favorite aunt Geny, we could watch the vendors at the local neighborhood market set up their stalls in the early mornings, several times a week.

Scouring the open markets for treasures, hand in hand with Vovo, is one of my fondest memories in life. On those market days, we would begin by making a mental note of what was needed. It was done by simply listing the items aloud. I was very young at the time, but I do not recall ever seeing her read or write. To this day, I love the adventure of searching out a good bargain and the exciting discovery of a unique item that will complete an outfit, grace my home, or bless a friend as a gift.

On market day, we were armed with Vovo's crocheted shopping bag and a small, safely concealed pocketbook containing a limited amount of money—Tia Geny's hard-earned money. Off we went, walking toward all the vibrant colors and sweet-smelling deals that only an outdoor market can provide.

Bartering is a skill born of experience and intuition. Vovo taught me to never buy anything at the offered price, to be aware of shopping traps, and to understand that everything is negotiable. She taught me to read a person's intentions and to be aware of his or her level of honesty and integrity. She taught me to be patient when bartering and to walk away when the time was right. She taught me to trust my feelings and my instincts during these open-market days.

Simple Clear-Sensing Lessons Vovo Taught Me

- ☐ When you first approach a vendor at the market, be aware of what your body tells you about the person or the market stand. Do you sense honesty? Goodness? Do they care about what they are selling? Are they selling with confidence and good intentions?
- ☐ If you feel unsettled or weak, walk away.
- ☐ If you feel excited or happy, wait until you calm ☐ down before bartering.
- ☐ If you feel calm and confident, barter with confidence!
- ☐ If you feel sick, tired, sad, or lonely, pray for them and walk on.

When you pay attention, you can pick up the vibrations of how another person feels. In fact, what you are doing is putting forth a more conscious effort toward empathy. Every day, without much effort, we notice how others feel, whether it is sad, feisty, angry, or any other of the numerous human emotions. This process is very natural to the majority of us. To heighten your clairsentient abilities is to increase this awareness of the other person's presence—*but without judgment.*

Now here is the kicker: Spiritual clear sensing is enhanced when you concentrate your efforts on awareness for the greater good of everyone concerned. In order to improve this ability to a pronounced level, you need to be available to support others as you feel called upon to do so; then you will become more sensitive. Be sure to understand that *it isn't about you.*

True spiritual empathy requires that we move out of judgment and self-centered concerns and into greater compassion toward others. At the market, Vovo taught me to pray for the person who was sad or didn't feel well. It was an act of kindness, easily completed for the greater good with the highest of intentions. The more kindness we spread, the greater our wisdom of clairsentience becomes.

To register more empathically, it is important to have a clear baseline of how you feel. Start from a calm, centered place within yourself before you begin evaluating someone else. Know first how you feel before you try approaching someone. Then you can pay attention to any changes you may experience in your own body as you come up to the person. The subtle shift in emotion and energy is usually related to the other person and not you. Holding a clear, loving intention will support successful determination of your experiences as a clairsentient.

Specifics Regarding Clairsentience

Did you ever experience a time when you felt the air was so thick you were suffocating? A time when you steered clear of a particular person or situation because they made you feel creepy? Perhaps you looked at a plate of food and didn't want to eat, simply because of the way it made you feel. These are intuitive, clairsentient nudges.

Many people have described feeling sick when they encountered a person who was ill, such as a coworker who shares an office space. On the way to work, the person feels normal, but as soon as they walk into the office, they get a headache or other pain or begin to feel nauseous. This is another example of clear sensing. The person is not sick, but the presence of someone else who is makes them feel as if they are.

Many of you, especially teachers and parents, can attest to the chain reaction that occurs when one youngster in a group of kids starts bouncing off the walls. Within a few minutes, half the room is antsy and fidgeting as well. How does this happen? We are all connected by subtle, irresistible vibes, especially the young and the unaware. We all share energy. We are all connected at the soul level where we match up on vibrational frequencies. It is beautiful and helpful to intuit where a person is truly coming from, and extrasensory awareness makes it possible.

In the marketplace, Vovo merely wanted the best and most nutritious food for our table, so she made use of her greater emotional potential to achieve that goal. In the classroom, a teacher needs to key in to the agitated child and support a transitional activity that will ward off an encroaching avalanche of naughty, disruptive kids. Perhaps a few moments of deep breathing can help or maybe a soft song played in the background. The person walking into a social setting will be all the more successful at meeting the partner of his or her dreams if they are aware of the energy and vibration of suitable people in the room. Clear sensing is useful, and it can be life affirming.

As you expand your awareness of others' emotional and physical states, please be sure you are not invading their privacy or openly expressing aloud your intuitive knowings and awareness. It is imperative to be ethical and conscientious of other people's privacy. If you sense that a person needs a hug and you know them well enough to offer one, first ask, "Do you need a hug?" If you don't know the person at all, it is best to say a quiet prayer and let God address his or her individual needs.

Yes, there are some popular shows airing today in which celebrity intuitives, mediums, or other spiritually gifted personalities approach people publically and announce aloud their psychic observations. That is television, not the real world. It is important to value and respect others and avoid drawing attention to yourself. Loving, compassionate spiritual work is not about you. It is about the directive of a higher power. We are the channels, the messengers, and the undercover angels.

This is the truth about why we have the gift of clairsentience: so we can experience one another as parts of ourselves, connected as brothers and sisters, and can pray for the highest good for us all. This is the calling on your soul: prayer, compassion, and, when it is right and good, action.

Sometimes you may be guided toward other types of good will. Just follow your heart and good intentions, and then be sure to act on

- [ ] what is good for God,
- [ ] what is good for others, and
- [ ] what is good for you.

Angel-Decoding Secret Key #8
The longer we are able to hold a positive thought and emotion, the more powerful the energy of the emotion becomes.

We are powerful towers of energy. Our bodies pick up a multitude of vibrations on a regular basis. Ever wonder how the voice from one cell phone travels to another? The cell phone first needs to be dialed into a specific frequency that connects it to a transmitting tower. Well, we are just like that cell phone when we dial into the higher frequencies of our intuitive abilities. God is the transmitting tower, and through God, we are consciously tapping into one another as needed to support and communicate with each other.

At times, we have to filter out the magnitude of feelings we encounter on a daily basis; it can be overwhelming to tune in to every radio station at once. Thus, we need to learn to be more selective. Many clairsentients are hypersensitive; they need to become experts at totally blocking out the barge of feelings in their presence. It is no wonder we often seem so self-absorbed because tuning out appears safer and calmer than the alternative. Remember, with a simple prayer you can release the overwhelming sensations and ask God and the angels to take care of the situation, person, or thing. Then you can let go of worry and allow the loving angels to do their work. In this way, you are doing great good unawares.

Tips for Receiving Clairsentient Messages

☐ Be centered, clear, positive, and aware.

☐ Drinking water supports clearer channels of intuition. Alcohol and other harmful substances cloud us.

☐ Emotional clearing and chakra balancing are optimal choices for cleansing your senses. Schedule regular sessions with a Reiki practitioner or energy healer or learn Reiki and practice on yourself.

☐ Eat healthful foods, as close to organic as possible. Organic foods carry a high vibration, and eating them aids in increased vibrational awareness and clarity.

☐ Always cut cords of connection to people or situations that are toxic. Simply call on the Archangel Michael to cut away cords of pain, sickness, negativity, stress, fear, or abuse, and repeat as needed.

☐ True clairsentient communication from loved ones and angels will feel warm, gentle, tingly, familiar, and loving.

☐ Goosebumps, hair tugs, tapping, and sudden sensations within your body are messages, especially when you have asked or prayed for a sign or guidance.

☐ The heart-to-heart connection lesson from Vovo really works! Focus on a person's name, and pay

63

attention to the subtle impressions you feel while connecting with their name.

☐ When praying for others, pray to God, but ask the angels to help as well. Archangel Raphael can support healing; Archangel Michael can bring protection, strength, and courage; Archangel Gabriel can support better communication.

☐ You can send love and healing with a prayer and positive intentions. Simply state a person's name, and imagine you are surrounding them with love and healing light from your heart to theirs. The Archangel Raphael and the Lord Jesus are known for their healing energy, so invoke their assistance in matters of healing.

☐ Use meditation, crystals, essential oils, flowers, plants, and water to calm and center as well as to amplify your spiritual awareness. Workshops offered by specialists in these areas can offer a wealth of information.

☐ Jot down your experiences in your angel-decoding journal or lexicon. Angels will repeat sensations of awareness in order to support your understanding and build your clairsentient vocabulary.

☐ Above all, be courageous! The world needs caring, clear-sensing people to help heal it. When in doubt, pray and send love from your heart to all living things.

Affirm daily: "Dear sweet, loving angels, guide me in discerning clear spiritual sensing for the greatest good. I am a loving, compassionate clairsentient!"

CHAPTER 8

More Than the Eye Can See

I decided that it was not wisdom that enabled poets to write
their poetry, but a kind of instinct or inspiration, such as
you find in seers and prophets who deliver all their sublime
messages without knowing in the least what they mean.

—Socrates

When I was quite young and before I started school,
Vovo was my lone companion during most of the
day. My aunt Geny was usually away at work. I didn't have
a lot of toys, and the only books in the apartment were filled
with words, not pictures. So, unknowingly, I entertained
angels to pass the time.

In reflection, it seems so natural that I played with the
gentle, colored lights that visited me almost daily. Young
and unassuming, I enjoyed hours of graceful company with
beautiful rays of light. Perhaps I was simply catching sunrays.
Yet I distinctly remember a deeper communication and a
sense of suspended time as I played with the angelic clouds.

Clairvoyance ~ Clear Vision

A widely misunderstood type of intuition is clairvoyance, or the ability to clearly see or conceptualize people, places, situations, and other things. *Clairvoyance* means "clear sight" or "clear seeing."(Encyclopedia Britannica, Phychology) It describes seeing spiritual forms as if they were physically present or receiving a visual impression in the mind's eye, similar to what we experience in a dream state. When we dream, our eyes are closed, and we see within our minds as opposed to using visual sight.

Clairvoyance can present in various forms, such as in dreams, momentary impressions, physical signs, angelic clouds, twinkly lights, colored mist, or sparkles. It is very likely that all of us have, at one time or another, thought we were seeing things, but upon closer inspection, whatever it was seemed to disappear. Many people mistakenly believe that clear spiritual vision means to see a three-dimensional image. This may be true for some, but most of us experience subtler forms of this intuitive ability. In order to support and comfort us, our angels wish to connect through any modality possible. Therefore, signs from the angels and our loved ones are abundantly showered upon us as gentle nudges and impressions. If you pay attention, you will notice a growing number of clairvoyant messages from your angels and spirit guides.

Here are some common examples of clairvoyant experiences:

☐ If you played with an imaginary friend when you were young, you were entertaining clairvoyant visual conceptions.

- ☐ If you dream while sleeping or daydream while awake, you are exercising your clairvoyant abilities.

- ☐ If you have seen sudden, sparkling lights that flash and disappear or the apparent emergence of a person/ presence out of the corner of your eye, you are capturing a clairvoyant moment.

- ☐ If numbers seem to be more prominently placed in your awareness—such as seeing the same numbers repeatedly on a digital clock or a license plate or as part of a phone number or address—these are signs.

- ☐ If you continually come across the same objects, such as feathers, coins, butterflies, eagles, and so on, while coincidently thinking about a loved one who has died, you are receiving a clear visual sign from beyond.

Opening the Door to Clairvoyance

Quiet meditation can enhance your abilities for and your awareness of the clairvoyant impressions in your life. Often, a regular meditative practice allows you to relax enough to move from the demanding world around you and into an open subconscious and less conspicuous mind. I encourage you again to use the centering-breath exercise described in chapter 1 to support your abilities here and to aid in expanding your inner knowing.

It is totally and completely safe for you to enhance your spiritual sight. Ask your angels to help you feel more confident and capable of seeing the signs of love and guidance they provide for you. Ask them to pave the way, to remove any unwarranted fears, and to support positive experiences. You are always in charge, so don't worry that you will start seeing things at every turn. You can control your extrasensory sight as needed like flipping a switch on and off. Your abilities will most likely build as you grow spiritually. Remember that in order to truly see God's loving messages, we must first feel love and genuinely want the same for others. As compassion and generosity grow within you, so will your abilities as an angel-decoding practitioner.

Activating Spiritual Sight

An important but also enjoyable way to begin awakening your clairvoyance is to open and stimulate the third eye, also known as the inner eye. Its location aligns with your pineal gland, located in the midbrain between the right and left hemispheres. This part of the brain supports multidimensional perception. The third eye is often referred to as the bridge leading to divine consciousness. I often picture it as a small movie screen appearing between my physical eyes where impressions and visions from within my mind are displayed.

Here are some suggestions to help you open and stimulate the third eye:

☐ Ask angels to remove any layers that may have accumulated and are now blocking your ability to spiritually see more clearly. Ask Archangel Raphael, whose focus is healing, to help heal any fear or limitations you have about spiritual sight.

☐ With help from your angels, imagine removing the gunk from the space between your eyes, the center of clairvoyance. As you do, use your actual, physical hand to reach up and clear away the space. The action is similar to removing a Band-Aid; just peel away anything blocking your spiritual sight.

☐ Affirm: "I clearly see God's love and welcome the gentle beauty of clairvoyant messages for the greatest good."

☐ Imagine the prevailing light of God's love and energy as it clears any misperceptions and enlightens your soul, like a powerful divine beam clearing your third eye.

☐ Find a place to lie down comfortably, and then put a clear, positively charged quartz crystal on the region of the third eye as you meditate or pray with the intention of opening the inner eye.

☐ Work to remove any toxins from your life. For example, fluoride, which appears in many modern-day products and accumulates and calcifies in the pineal gland. Eat healthfully, and lovingly care for your body and soul.

☐ Consider training as a Reiki practitioner; the attunement process is an excellent way to clear and balance your energy centers.

☐ Affirm: "I am clairvoyant."

Catching a View of Auras

An aura can be described as an emanating energy field surrounding each living thing, and an emerging clairvoyant skill is the ability to see auras. To practice the skill, relax and pay close attention to the soft lights and vibrations surrounding objects and people. Hold a soft gaze, similar to how you unfocus your eyes to see those Magic Eye pictures containing hidden, three-dimensional images. In fact, I have used the Magic Eye photos in my workshops to help teach emerging clairvoyants how to hold a relaxed visual stare in order to see auras around people, animals, and other things more effectively. The pictures are fun and easy to use.

If you hold this soft gaze and concentrate on the energy surrounding an individual, an aura, or a luminous radiation, will often be subtly exposed. Every living thing has an aura. Ever notice how on a sunny or very bright day, the colors of plants and all of nature appear more vibrant? I enjoy holding a soft gaze around the foliage, and by doing so, I can easily see that each petal has its own unique layer of colored lights emanating beyond the physical portion of the leaf or petal. Holding a soft gaze as you look at someone's head, especially when they are against a white background, will often reveal an outline or aura color, even to the eye of a novice.

Auras are fun to see, but they are even more interesting to interpret. When I begin working personally with a client, their aura is what I first see, often before any other impression from the reading has been shared. The various aura colors imply deeper meanings of the individual's state of mind, physical health, or even intentions and integrity.

There are various aura charts on the market these days to substantiate meaning to an aura reading. However, I find that your angels will use your frame of reference to support further meaning. If you are patient and dedicated to practicing, you will find that you can attribute clearer, more precise definitions to the aura colors of any individual and form your own interpretation with the help of your angels.

The appendix has a list of aura colors and their meanings. This chart can be used as a guide when you first begin investigating auras. I highly encourage you to use all of your intuitive senses as you compose an aura reading. Don't rely simply on color or the definitions put on a chart created by someone else, including me.

An aura is dynamic, just like you, which means the colors will change from day to day, even moment to moment. A novice can read the colors that currently surround an individual, but as your abilities grow, you will see more deeply and begin to grasp the individual more holistically. You will be able to read the character of their most prominent aura. When skillfully combining all of your intuitive faculties, you will discover much more information than meets the eye. When reading another person and having the greatest of intentions and care for their well-being, you will find that the angels will pour forth sensations, knowings, visualizations, and whispers with abounding blessings.

You cannot succeed in this process without having the highest vibration of love toward those with whom you are working. Remember, messages and meanings work through you to support others; they should not come from you or your opinions. True angel readings are a product of the Creator's love; you are simply the go-between, the messenger. Deliver these messages with the highest of intentions and in the most humble manner. If you are unsure, ask for clarity, say a prayer, and share what comes from the highest of vibrations: love.

True Characteristics of Dream Visitations

Dreams have been clearly documented as a medium of communication with departed loved ones. Many people have vivid dreams in which they experience a meeting, interaction, or visitation with a deceased loved one. Dream visitations are commonly vivid in nature and are usually combined with an important message or intense emotion. Our loved ones, angels, and spirit guides can more easily communicate with us when our conscious mind is at rest and our subconscious mind is open to the subtle wonder of spiritual interface.

The following are general qualifications of true dream visitations:

- □ The person or animal appears to be real and vivid.
- □ You remember the dream very clearly and recall explicit details.

☐ The characteristics of the visiting person or animal are loving, healthy, and caring—never scary, hurtful, or punishing.

☐ You feel reassured and sense their message clearly. They may not speak, but you know and understand what has been conveyed.

☐ Visitation dreams can bring cautions and warnings. However, messages will be delivered in a supportive and productive manner.

Here are some guidelines for divine communication through dreams:

☐ You can ask either consciously or unconsciously for an opportunity to connect with your loved one in dreamland. This is an excellent tool for those who are deeply grieving or who have unanswered questions about where their loved ones are or how they are doing.

☐ You may also experience a dream visitation from your guardian angel or a pronounced spirit guide. Guides usually bring life-affirming or life-directive messages because the dreamer is in need of guidance or has been praying for clarity.

☐ I highly recommend referring to a dream dictionary to support your understanding of dream symbols and metaphors.

Not all dreams are to be taken at face value. Prayer is a powerful way to balance any concerns that may derive from puzzling dreams. Recurring dreams are often a call from your subconscious to deal more directly with a nagging issue. Be open to seeking professional support with life issues and concerns, which may be overwhelming your day-to-day life. Professional counselors and psychologists are trained and educated to provide direct support for life's greatest problems and strategies to cope with them. Take excellent care of your greatest resource: you.

Tips for Awareness of Clairvoyant Messages

- ☐ Explore the major themes and symbols in your dreams by cross-referencing them with a dream dictionary, and add them to your angel-decoding glossary.
- ☐ Make note of recurring symbols, as they are clear messages.
- ☐ Number symbols have clear messages (see chapter 9).
- ☐ Twinkling lights, colored mist, and angelic clouds are physical signs of angelic presence. Be open to intuitively asking your angels what they mean.
- ☐ Impressions often show up during meditation. Include these impressions in your angel-decoding lexicon/ glossary with your own definitions or interpretations. The angels are teaching you their language by using your frame of reference and the world you see around you, so take note.
- ☐ Take care of your health, and keep your energy balanced for optimal success.
- ☐ Avoid harmful substances at all costs, for they poison your body and cloud your spiritual sight.

- ☐ True clairvoyance will not present if you are under the influence of alcohol, drugs, or other psychotropic substances. Visions occurring when under the influence do not qualify as clairvoyance.
- ☐ Clairvoyance is an amazing gift and a skill that will improve with patience and awareness. Faith in God, trust in your abilities, and moral discernment are vital to angel communication.

Use the contents of this chapter on clairvoyance to bridge a broader range of your visual abilities, both concretely—such as paying attention to numbers that may convey messages—and abstractly—such as listening to the messages of dreams and the interpretation of one's aura. I encourage you to add the vocabulary of impressions to your angel-decoding lexicon/glossary.

Remember that the art of journaling your dreams and other visions is vital to building your sixth-sensory abilities. Clinical observations have found that the subconscious mind appears to work in a cyclical manner, so taking note of and actively journaling your insights will demonstrate consistency throughout your experiences. This steady stream of information can provide firm support and a guiding light to live by.

Angel-Decoding Secret Key #9

Angelic messages are always encouraging, consistent, and never hurtful. Angels will work to send you the same important message or answer you are seeking in many forms.

A Vision Brings Peace

I have been privy to many stories involving angels, deceased loved ones, and miraculous, unexplainable experiences. My clients often worry that they are losing their minds because of their visions. They believe they have seen loved ones who died or have sensed the presence of the deceased in some other way. A woman who had lost her husband shared the following story.

It had been only a few months since her spouse's death, and Mary had been praying for a sign from heaven that he had made a successful transition to the other side. Struggling with grief, she picked up the Bible and began searching its pages for comfort. Between intervals of reading and weeping, she prayed. She whispered her hope into the lonely night surrounding her. Sitting stoically in a cozy chair situated in her bedroom, she noticed a warm, soft glow begin to fill the doorway to the hall. Staring in disbelief, she instantly recognized the distinct outline of her husband's frame. She explained to me that she intuitively understood his message, as opposed to hearing him speak aloud. He shared with her that his presence was meant to soothe her, that he was compassionate about her grief, yet also joyous in his new existence. She could not recall how long her experience lasted, only that she felt strangely comforted and more peaceful than she had in months.

We have been taught that seeing is believing, yet we have also been taught that we can't see spirit. Perhaps the idea of not seeing spirit has become archaic, especially in this day of instant access and an abundance of technological gadgets.

It is understood that scientists will soon develop equipment capable of filming fields of etheric energy. At the present time, Kirlian photography has been used to photograph the human aura, which is better known as the electromagnetic field or the human energy field. Since we can photograph the aura, perhaps capturing spiritual energy on film will be a possibility in the near future. For my client, experiencing the presence of her deceased husband was confirmation enough that seeing brings belief.

The Smiling iPad

Recently, I was in session with a client who had lost her cousin in a car accident. Through the process of mediumship, I connected with her departed loved one and promptly saw a huge smile. The client was immediately grateful for this first impression, as it seemed to confirm the true nature of her cousin and related to an experience she herself believed to be a message from heaven.

On a particularly difficult day of grieving for her cousin, Laura wrote a status on her Facebook page: "It would do me good just to see your smile." Then she went about her day. Later that same day, she heard a *thunk* as something fell to the floor in her room. Upon investigating, she saw her iPad, encased in its grip case, lying on the dusty floor. Somehow it had fallen from its secure spot on top of the dresser. She bent to pick it up, and in the dust was a huge smiley face, miraculously formed by the fallen iPad and its case. Laura believed this was the smile from her departed loved one that she had asked for. Miracles happen everyday, and our loved ones are never far from our hearts.

A Moment in Time

Suddenly, I saw into the future. Our world was finally, harmoniously blended and weaved, the best of all traditions, ethnicities, strengths, and ambitions elegantly combined into a single tapestry of human existence. My senses filled with a colorful, rhythmic, palatable vibration encompassing every musical genre imaginable. I witnessed people smiling and laughing, joyously reaching out to one another, and wordlessly inviting a heart-to-heart interface.

When this happened to me, I wasn't having an out-of-body experience. I was simply standing at my kitchen sink, rinsing out a dish. This timeless impression flashed momentarily in my mind's eye, yet it existed endlessly in spirit. Comprehensively compacted into perhaps a ten-second slice of my day, the vision appeared as a time warp where space expanded and the moment slowed and lingered. I could see, feel, hear, and understand that what I was experiencing was at some point in the future. I also understood that our current progress in technology was the catalyst for the eventual blending of the four corners of the earth. I felt we were finally emotionally, spiritually, and viscerally connected as a people. This vision gave me great hope for the course of humanity.

Affirm daily: "I see the beauty of the people and the world around me. I am profoundly clairvoyant!"

CHAPTER 9

On a Mission

Angels transcend every religion, every philosophy, every creed. In fact angels have no religion as we know it . . . their existence precedes every religious system that has ever existed on earth.

—Saint Thomas Aquinas

Exploring your spirituality, opening to your intuition, and professing your faith in God and the angels are the essence of angel decoding. If you are like me, you have a burning desire within you to make this world better and to help her people toward a joyful existence. Start by creating happiness right inside your own mind and heart. Peace begins within. The essence of our soul and true enlightenment is not somewhere outside ourselves. It is within and coincides with our divine purpose.

Happiness and peace are truly a mind-set, a practice, an understanding. Life can be cruel, and we can be fragile, but with faith we persevere. I choose to reach out to God and the angels to lift my spirit and lighten my load. More often, the angels will remind me in those moments to extend love, care, and compassion toward others and teach them to offer the same—to pay it forward in a never-ending circle of miracles.

You can decide to make your life amazing by choosing the mind-set of peace. Thoughts are things, and we build the future with progressively new ideas. Be conscious of your thoughts, and create the brightest future. We are all here on earth to learn from one another, to listen and care for each other, to show compassion, practice forgiveness, and reach out every day to love someone, anyone. This is truly our purpose in life. Purpose is not a career, a job, an occupation. Purpose is more relevant to matters of passion, drive, determination, and heart. Purpose is closer to a mission of the soul as we advocate for humanity through compassion and care of one another.

Believe in miracles, the amazing power of prayer, the trustworthiness of our angels, and the unity of our souls. A shift in consciousness and confidence will occur once you learn to trust the guidance within you and embrace the subtle assurance that comes from communicating with your angels. An allegiance to your divine purpose, the true authentic direction of your life, will be made clear as you steer faithfully and knowingly with God's grace.

I choose to see the Creator's light in each of us. I challenge you to practice compassion and in doing so to find inner peace. The world will never reach peace until each of us has established inner peace.

Epilogue

Final Ponderings

The plain fact is that the planet does not need more successful people. But it does desperately need more peacemakers, healers, restorers, storytellers, and lovers of every kind. It needs people who live well in their places. It needs people of moral courage willing to join the fight to make the world habitable and humane. And these qualities have little to do with success as we have defined it.

—David Orr, *Ecological Literacy*

Spiritual friends, please listen to the gentle nudges of your soul. If you were guided to read this book, you are a "lightworker," a spiritual sage of our time, a healer, restorer, peacemaker, and storyteller. You are the hope of our future as a united planet. Open your heart to your truth, and courageously step into your sacred power. Apply the lessons of this book to support a greater communication with your angels and spirit guides so you can have clarity in living a more authentic life.

There is no need to "work" at spiritual awareness—you are already blessed with it—but now is the time to embrace it. Just a few minutes of quiet meditation, centered breathing, and genuine prayer and intention can direct your daily path. Allow the flow of positive energy to support you while doors open to new possibilities of hope and opportunity. We are children of God, blessed with creative energy, supported by his angels and the guidance of our ancestors. Become the way, the truth, and the light of the Creator's purest intentions for this planet.

Take responsibility for Mother Earth, and take diligent care of yourself. Build strong, supportive relationships with the people in your life who resonate with the highest vibration of love and integrity for the greater good. Cease judgment, and choose loving action and compassion instead. Begin to replace synthetics with natural substances, and switch from processed/chemical matter to organic matter in your diet and your wares. Escape the limitations of your life. If you feel stuck or dissatisfied, awaken to your true calling. Find beauty and appreciate the present moment wherever life may take you, for nothing is more powerful than a soul ablaze with inspiration.

Angel–Decoding Secret Key #10
To obey the logic of your soul is the only path you need. You are masterful beyond knowing; you only need to heed the music of your heart.

Blessings and angel hugs!

Please visit me at www.MariaPeth.com

Twitter: @AngelicMaria444

FaceBook: Angelic Enlightenment

Blog: AngelicMaria.wordpress.com

Appendix

Aura Colors: A Basic Guide

white: honest, loyal, truthful, of a pure state, integrity

red: determined energy, feisty, powerful, negotiator, advocator, marketer

yellow: student, learner, intellect, inspirational, awakening

murky or dirty yellow: stressed, strained, overwhelmed

pink: nurturer, compassionate, caring, potential need for care and nurturing as well

hot pink: passion and drive, determination, in love

green: healer, naturalist, growth, nature oriented

purple: intuitive, visual, an emerging visionary, sensitive

orange: creative, changes on the way, transition, transformation, adventurer

blue: communicator, arts oriented, teacher, manager, guide

gold: Christ energy, leader, healer, teacher, counselor, truth, enlightenment

silver: abundance, surrounded by angels, new ideas, powerful ideas

gray: foggy, feeling blocked, sickness, deep sadness

black: heavy feelings, feeling down, unforgiving, confused

rainbow: hopeful, good things to come, Reiki healer, energy healer

earth colors: grounded, connected to the outdoors, nature, and animals

The Secret of Numbers

Have you ever had one of those days where number sequences keep showing up? You look at the clock and see 4:44 or 3:33 or 1:11. A car pulls up in front of you, and there it is again, a license plate with 777 or 222. According to Doreen Virtue, PhD, in her book *Angel Numbers 101,* repetitive number sequences have meaning and often bring messages from our angels.

I have found, more often than not, that the code of reading angel numbers offers me simple amusement at times, but it can also guide me in a joyful direction in life. This method of entertainment and guidance often puts a smile on my face and can turn my perspective in a positive direction. So are you wondering what some of the numbers may mean?

I will let you in on a few tips from Dr. Virtue's book. However, there are 999 number combinations, and I don't have them all memorized! But if you are interested in making new connections by using numbers and can keep an open mind about how your angels communicate with you, this may be fun and amazing for you.

Here is the scoop on a few of the numbers you may see:

- ☐ 1 represents the idea of keeping your thoughts positive. Your thoughts are powerful, so be kind to yourself and think positively.
- ☐ 2 represents the idea of "keeping the faith." Remember, when two or more are gathered in his name, he too is present.
- ☐ 3 represents the ascended masters, as in the Holy Trinity, including Christ. Know that the masters are with you and you are blessed.

See how logical some of these representations are? It's as if you always knew them, but now you can use and apply this concept to improve your life and catch a holy moment here and there. Let's keep going:

- ☐ 4 is my favorite, for it represents the angels and acts as a reminder that they are always with me. When I see 444, I know that the Creator is letting me know the angels are all around, a very comforting and joyful occurrence, which I am always grateful to acknowledge.

- ☐ 5 represents the idea that things are about to change for the better. Or it may appear to encourage you to speed ahead with an idea that you may be working on and to hold on tight for new possibilities.
- ☐ 6 is a call to balance—your day, your life, or even your checkbook.
- ☐ 7 is an accolade, saying, "Keep up the good work!"
- ☐ 8 is a number of abundance, fruition, and good fortune.
- ☐ And finally, 9 represents the idea of getting to work. More precisely, to work helping each other and focusing on the whole of humanity. A pretty big charge to take on, don't you think? A noble and grand idea!

Dr. Virtue's book goes into much more detail than what I've included here, and it is a useful reference in my line of work. I have found that people welcome the book as a gift, as they enjoy looking up the sequences that appear in their lives most regularly.

Of course, you don't need a book to connect with your angels. All you need is a little faith and the knowing that we are all blessed with many gifts from our Creator, through whom all things are possible. So 111 to all of you and 222— in other words, stay positive and keep the faith.

Calling on Love: Meditation and Affirmations to Enhance Claircognizance

Sit or lie comfortably. Take a deep breath. Breathe in tranquility and light. Breathe out stress, negativity, and anger. Breathe in love, harmony, and truth. Breathe out pain and frustration. Breathe in peace, light, and happiness. Breathe out all negativity.

Now affirm:

> I am peaceful, centered, and joyful.
> I am tranquil.
> I am light.
> I am harmony.
> I am love.
> I am remarkable.
> I am a channel of truth.
> I am clear, honest, loyal, and true!

Imagine the light of the Creator reaching to your heart, your soul, and your spirit. Unite with the Creator's love and with universal truth. Imagine being one with spirit. The light of truth fills your heart with pure love. Your energy is abundant. You are filled with love.

You feel comfortable, safe, and blessed with universal understanding. Your awareness of spirit is clear, sharp, and amazingly accurate. All the answers you are calling forth are available to you. All the knowing, all the truth, is available for you. You are able to discern information for the greatest good. You are clear, loving, and safe.

Rest for several minutes, basking in the light of the Creator's love. Be open to receiving unconditional love and channeling that love to others. Be open to knowing. Be open to the truth of God's greatest intentions. Allow yourself to be a vessel of angelic truth. Continue to breathe deeply and in the frequency of love.

Divine guidance from our angels is a blessing. Trust your inspirational moments, and be open to the loving, holistic understandings that you are blessed with today and always.

Prayers

Prayer for Healing

Precious Jesus and healing angels, surround me with your healing presence. Lift the hurt, the suffering, and erase the unbearable pain. Wrap me in your golden light of precious love and wipe away the bitterness. I accept your loving blessings, and I am grateful for your power. Please fill my broken body with your saving grace. And so it is.

Prayer for Guidance

Beautiful Lord, sweet angels, Holy Spirit, I ask for your loving guidance regarding _____. I pray for certainty, clarity, and clear discernment in all I do and all I am. I know you are with me in every moment, and I pray to fully awaken to your loving direction. Help me to feel your steadfast presence. Help me to face the greatest challenges by holding strong to the wisdom of your light on the road to faith. So be it.

Prayer to Help Heal a Broken Heart

God of power and grace, my heart is crushed and deeply mangled. My wounds are jagged with no promise of hope. Please touch my soul with your light, and bring healing for my broken heart. Send love and healing light to all concerned in all directions to the ends of the universe. I accept your loving support and accept that I am whole and will completely heal in your presence. I ask for this through all of time and space, especially now. Amen.

Prayer for Love

Sweet loving God and heavenly angels, I am open to allowing the perfect relationships into my life. I accept love and am deserving of uniting with others who will honor and respect me as I honor and respect them. I am open to healthy, loving, and compassionate love. Amen.

Maria's Heart
Centered Meditation

Sit comfortably with your back, neck and head aligned. Place your hands on your heart and imagine you see the person you most want to connect to. This person can be living or one who is deceased. Perhaps you want to "check in" with someone whom you love, who lives a distance from you. Perhaps you want to see if you can get a message from a loved one who has crossed-over.

Begin by taking several deep breaths and quietly repeating the name of the person you desire to connect to. Create a peaceful harmonious inner world while maintaining loving memories and thoughts.

As you breathe, fill your heart with love and allow the highest intentions to flow through you, with you and for you.

Take note of new sensations, visions, thoughts, or knowings, which you perceive. The connection and impressions may be subtle, yet miraculously revealing.

Don't worry if you don't seem to notice anything the first few times you try this exercise, as deeper and richer awareness will come with practice and time.

Miracles happen every day.

ABOUT THE AUTHOR

Maria Gurney Peth PhD

Maria Gurney Peth, PhD, is a spiritual teacher, angel therapist, intuitive life coach and angel decoding specialist, in high demand for her ability to connect with the angelic realm. Maria has worked with thousands of satisfied clients in personal consulting sessions, life-affirming workshops, and retreats. People are drawn to Maria's genuine sincerity and natural intuitive abilities. Clients book sessions for the magic and leave with solid strategies to support a centered and blessed life.

Born in Brazil, Maria was separated from her mother at a young age. In the early 1960s, telephones were not a standard feature in every South American home. Through the grace and teaching of her Brazilian grandmother, Maria awakened to her spiritual gifts, embracing intuitive methods for connecting with her mother, who was living more than 5,000 miles away.

Maria believes in living authentically, soulfully, and with purpose. She is a life-empowering spiritual teacher and coach, on a mission to demystify the idea of communicating with angels, and champions the ease with which the skill of intuition can be learned. The passion she brings to working with her angels has been a mainstay of her personal spiritual journey. She believes miracles happen every day.

Maria has earned degrees from the University of Iowa and the University of Denver, with a focus on education and social psychology. She earned her doctorate from the American Institute of Holistic Theology in metaphysics. Maria is a published writer, motivational speaker, and gifted teacher.

Formal business: Angelic Enlightenment -offers: "Inspiration for your soul and guidance for your life."

Connect with Maria on: Twitter @AngelicMaria444, Connect on Facebook –Angelic Enlightenment Website: www.MariaPeth.com

Made in the USA
Middletown, DE
18 August 2015